The Secret Lore
of Gardening

Marie-Louise von Franz, Honorary Patron

**Studies in Jungian Psychology
by Jungian Analysts**

Daryl Sharp, General Editor

The Secret Lore of Gardening

Patterns of Male Intimacy

Graham Jackson

To my Zürich analysts, France Amerongen and John Hill,
and to William Arthur Kimber.

Canadian Cataloguing in Publication Data

Jackson, Graham. 1949-
The secret lore of gardening: patterns of male intimacy

(Studies in Jungian psychology by Jungian analysts; 52)

Includes bibliographical references and index.

ISBN 0-919123-53-8

1. Homosexuality, Male—Psychological aspects.
2. Gay men—Psychology.
3. Jung, C.G. (Carl Gustav), 1875-1961.
I. Title. II. Series.

HQ76.J33 1991   306.76'62   C91-094611-6

INNER CITY BOOKS
Box 1271, Station Q, Toronto, Canada M4T 2P4
Telephone (416) 927-0355
FAX 416-924-1814

Honorary Patron: Marie-Louise von Franz.
Publisher and General Editor: Daryl Sharp.
Senior Editor: Victoria Cowan.

INNER CITY BOOKS was founded in 1980 to promote the
understanding and practical application of the work of C.G. Jung.

Cover: "Yellow Man, Green Man," oil painting by Gerard Gauci (© 1991).

Index by Daryl Sharp

Printed and bound in Canada by John Deyell Company

Contents

See last page for other titles by Inner City Books

Hamo Thornycroft, *The Mower,* 1884
(Walker Art Gallery, Liverpool)

1
Introduction

Mankind has always been concerned with the question of the opposites—their separation and reconciliation. However they have been formulated—as good and evil, light and darkness, upper and lower, chaos and order, yin and yang, etc.— the tension between them has been an inevitable given of the universal condition. Jung recognized this war of seemingly irreconcilable opposites as the "ineradicable and indispensable [precondition] of psychic life";[1] without the tension of opposites, individuation could not go forward. Out of it comes, according to Jung, a third possibility, irrational in nature, bewildering to the conscious mind: the symbol.

For Jung, consciousness and unconsciousness were the main opposing forces of psychic life. Assuming only a marginally smaller role in his description of such phenomena were the opposites of male and female. The classical Jungian view even defines conscious and unconscious as male and female respectively. In Jung's formulation of the process of psychic development to which he gave the name individuation, the journey to the Self was made possible only through the mediation or intercession of the contrasexual component of the personality, the anima or animus, those archetypal personifications of male and female. For a man seeking ultimate understanding, the anima was said to function somewhat like Beatrice in the *Paradiso* of Dante; she it is who makes it all possible. She is a soul-image, a not-I; she is the Other who facilitates the inner journey.

Without wishing here to debate this model of the "interior landscape," as Martha Graham so aptly termed it—and I do find it highly debatable—I take issue with a conclusion frequently drawn by analytical psychologists—particularly, but not exclusively, of the classical school—namely that, to quote but one, "Complete realisation and integration of [the anima] *requires* partnership with the opposite sex."[2]

If that were true, vast numbers of people, among them priests, monks, bachelors and homosexual men, would be deprived of not only satisfactory contact

---

[1] Jung, *Mysterium Coniunctionis,* CW 14, par. 206. [CW refers throughout to *The Collected Works of C.G. Jung]*

[2] Andrew Samuels, et al. *A Critical Dictionary of Jungian Analysis,* p. 23 (emphasis added). It is worth noting here, as Jungian analyst John Beebe reminds us in "Toward an Image of Male Partnership," that Jung described the anima as the archetype of life, not of love. ("Archetypes of the Collective Unconscious," *The Archetypes and the Collective Unconscious,* CW 9i, par. 66)

with their soul but also access to the Self. They would remain arrested or stunted in their psychic development.

Such an accusation has in fact long been leveled against homosexual men by many schools of psychology, which insist on the homosexual's chronic tie to Mom. Jung himself borrowed from Freud's ideas on the aetiology of homosexuality and, with slight modifications in terminology, he too presented it as a mother-based neurosis in which the anima-soul remains confused with mother and the man remains forever a son (and never, therefore, an adult).[3] Out of this thinking arose the identification of homosexual with puer, and vice versa, to the detriment in understanding of both.

For some other Jungians, homosexuality has been seen as a shadow problem, linked, of course, to an incomplete separation from mother and her castrating animus.[4] Barbara Hannah, for instance, wrote that "a great many cases of homosexuality or other apparently absurd over- and undervaluations of some member of the same sex are due [to the fascination exerted by the shadow]."[5] Thus, in the area of homosexuality, analytical psychology has shown itself quite capable of the same kind of reductionism/causalism (albeit expressed in a quasi-mystical language) as the Freudian school; not only that, it demonstrates thereby its own want of faith in the workings of the unconscious and its archetypal imagery.

Rafael Lopez-Pedraza has written elegantly of how a "sorcerer's apprentice" has wreaked havoc with the psychological understanding of homosexuality by means of paradigms which have

---

[3] Jung did, however, see a positive side to a man's mother complex, as follows:

"[He] may have a finely differentiated Eros instead of, or in addition to, homosexuality. . . . This gives him a great capacity for friendship, which often creates ties of astonishing tenderness between men and may even rescue friendship between the sexes from the limbo of the impossible. He may have good taste and an aesthetic sense which are fostered by the presence of a feminine streak. Then he may be supremely gifted as a teacher because of his almost feminine insight and tact. He is likely to have a feeling for history, and to be conservative in the best sense and cherish the values of the past. Often he is endowed with a wealth of religious feelings, which help to bring the *ecclesia spiritualis* into reality; and a spiritual receptivity which makes him responsive to revelation." ("Psychological Aspects of the Mother Complex," *The Archetypes and the Collective Unconscious,* CW 9i, par. 164)

What is particularly striking about this passage with its emphasis on the positive face of homoeros is not its content, which is, to say the least, curious, but rather its rarity in Jung's and Jungian writing.

[4] Jungians have taken many different approaches to male homosexuality and homoeroticism, ranging from senex-puer to hermaphrodite and androgyne. I do not intend to survey this, mostly patronizing, literature here. Interested readers may refer to Robert Hopcke, *Jung, Jungians and Homosexuality.*

[5] *Striving Towards Wholeness,* p. 19.

placed homosexuality within a sterile causalism that tries to understand it in terms of the father and mother. Western culture has evidently lost contact with the archetypes which are behind eros among men. Thus an archetypal view of homo-erotica has been falsified. Psychology's conceptual coinages are word-facades rendered out of "scientific" fantasies but, in reality, they are a cover for a basic component in the history of Western culture. Without wishing to value-judge the scientific approach, it nevertheless occludes the perspective toward tracking down other archetypes that, during a lifetime, can take over men's relationships.[6]

To be fair to Hannah, she does describe the shadow as "those missing pieces of ourselves that remind us unconsciously of our lost wholeness."[7] Whether she intended it or not, she thus credits the homosexual relationship with the potential for reconciling its partners with Self. This idea has been developed by Anthony Stevens, who refutes the exclusive position of the anima (and heterosexual partnership) in relation to soul, spirit and Self.[8] He concludes: "The heterosexual bond is not *de rigueur*. There is not only one road to Rome."[9] Even Jung, while expressing the view that homosexuality suggests an "incomplete detachment from the hermaphroditic archetype, coupled with a distinct resistance to identify with the role of a one-sided sexual being," adds a qualification:

Such a disposition should not be adjudged negative in all circumstances, in so far as it preserves the archetype of the Original Man, which a one-sided sexual being has, up to a point, lost.[10]

The basis for such ideas is actually a very old one. It can be located in several passages of Plato's writings, but nowhere more graphically than in Aristophanes' speech in *The Symposium*. Aristophanes depicts humans as originally round (read: whole) beings, some composed of male and female halves, and some of two female or two male halves. These beings became arrogant over time and, to punish them, Zeus cut them in half. Out of pity for them he then rearranged their reproductive organs so that the two separated creatures might have some means of reconnecting with or of imitating their former, lost wholeness. Later in the evening's presentations, Socrates himself takes the view that "love exists only in relation to some object, and . . . that object must be something of which he is at present in want."[11] That object, Socrates adds, is not just the beautiful

---

[6] *Hermes and His Children,* p. 77.

[7] *Striving Towards Wholeness,* p. 19.

[8] *Archetype: A Natural History of the Self,* pp. 198-199.

[9] Ibid., p. 199.

[10] "Concerning the Archetypes and the Anima Concept," *The Archetypes and the Collective Unconscious,* CW 9i, par. 146.

[11] *The Symposium,* pp. 77-78.

and the good, but also the immortal[12] and the route to this end begins with the love for young men.

The Symposium gives us a metaphorical as well as philosophical basis for approaching homosexual relationship (between men anyway) as a relationship to the Other, the not-I or not-yet-I, involving the opposites, both in separation and in reconciliation. Barbara Hannah, in spite of herself perhaps, hinted at this; Anthony Stevens most definitely makes it a question of ego and Self dynamics. Peter Schellenbaum, in a recent work, seems also to have been inspired by Plato. He writes:

> It happens occasionally that I meet someone whose personality is exactly what still slumbers in my soul's unconscious. Then the need stirs in me to connect with this person so that in being one with the other I learn to develop the still undeveloped sides of myself that the other lives consciously and openly. . . . I communicate with the other in this realm that already constitutes a mature, central domain of his or her personality, which is timely for me to develop just now. I communicate with the other as in a mirror because I see mirrored in the other's personality this realm of which I knew little or nothing up until now.[13]

With these ideas in mind I want to examine homosexual relationships as aiming at wholeness. I do not want to argue homosexuality from a causal point of view. I feel that this is impossible, and soul-destroying. Rather I will concentrate on certain of the images, fantasies, metaphors—in short, the archetypal background—of male homosexual relationships. I am interested also in homo-erotic relationships, that is, attraction between men that is not acted out sexually, but these I will try to distinguish from clearly homosexual phenomena. Such a distinction is a question only of degree; after all, the motivating force, union with the same sex, is identical in each.

When one looks for material that discusses the kinds of polarity found in homosexual relationships, one invariably finds oneself in a cul-de-sac. Contemporary psychological literature on homosexuality confines itself for the most part either to reminting "conceptual coinages" of the masters or to analyzing the interactions of the homosexual person with his social environment. Occasionally, as in the following passage, psycho-sociological analysis raises the question of role models, which pertains on some level to our interest in polarity within the homosexual relationship:

> Gay male couples usually have no reliable relationship role models to pattern themselves after or, indeed, to avoid patterning themselves after. Those couples who try to follow the traditional heterosexual models of marriage

---

[12] Ibid., p. 87.

[13] *How To Say No to the One You Love,* p. 120.

invariably find themselves unable to survive the rigidities imposed by the gender-related expectations. Male couples do not function as husband and wife with one assuming one role and the other the other. Gradually some models are evolving in our literature and theatre, but all too often even these models are following old stereotypes of the "butch-fem" genre.[14]

What emerges here is a concern with finding a more meaningful guide to the fulfillment of one's basic identity. Unfortunately, as with most, if not all, of this literature, the guide is seldom sought in the land of archetypes. Such writers as McWhirter and Mattison (authors of the extract cited above) assume, their nods to literature and theater notwithstanding, that it is all a matter for conscious management.

C.A. Tripp takes up the theme of polarity in homosexual relationships in a way that echoes Socrates' notion of love's object representing something the lover perceives himself to lack:

> The homosexual, like everyone else, usually manages to develop his own assets to the point of becoming reasonably satisfied with them; what he wants to import are the differing qualities which have made his partner attractive. Thus the items of highest import-priority are characteristically those which a person has never tried to develop on his own.[15]

Tripp concludes this paragraph by insisting that "notions to the effect that the homosexual is looking for some narcissistic reflection of his own image are as mythical . . . as Narcissus himself."[16] In a later chapter, he gives examples of what he means by polarity, and we are disappointed to discover that, for him, it is confined to persona differences:

> It is not unusual to find homosexual relationships in which such chasms [as age, race, background, social level] are bridged with ease. Sometimes the contrast between partners is enormous: the man of letters and the stevedore, a newscaster and a Japanese chef, the professional man and a construction worker, a biochemist and a truck driver. It is as if a fundamental rapport between same-sex partners not only permits them to hurdle social distances but often to be especially stimulated by them.[17]

Certainly, the point Tripp makes about the homosexual capacity to tolerate differences is an interesting one, containing political ramifications that belong to the landscape I propose to explore.

Most thorough in his exploration of polarity within a homosexual context

---

[14] Emery S. Hetrick and Terry S. Stein, *Innovations in Psychotherapy with Homosexuals*, p. 128.

[15] *The Homosexual Matrix*, p. 97.

[16] Ibid., p. 98.

[17] Ibid., p. 168.

was the late New York psychiatrist Paul Rosenfels.[18] He divided homosexual men into assertive and yielding types. Psychological health, he maintained, could be achieved only through recognition of one's type and subsequent specialization. The domain or specialty of the assertive type is power (in a Marsian sense) and of the yielding type, love (Venusian, in other words). Each of these types is irresistibly drawn to the other and, through relationship, comes not to an incorporation or integration of the qualities of the opposite or not-I (as a Jungian might expect), but to a refinement of his own type. The fruit of the relationship between assertive and yielding types is the enhanced creative potential of each. Rosenfels' ideas, although expressed in dense and difficult prose, provoke much thought; his idea of enhanced creativity, in particular, belongs to this work as well.

There are two basic configurations of homosexual relationship: the older man-younger man configuration, which inevitably involves the education or initiation of the latter and sometimes of the former as well; and the brothers- or comrades-in-arms relationship, that is, one between equals and having a heroic goal or task. Embracing both is a polarity I describe as green-yellow. Though the description may strike the reader as unfamiliar, even strange, green and yellow men have felt a mutual attraction at least since Gilgamesh and Enkidu first wrestled each other to a realization of their equality: "In the silence of the people they began to laugh / And clutched each other in their breathless exaltation."[19] The mythology, legends, fairy tales, literature, theater, dance and art of many cultures following that of ancient Uruk fairly burst with examples of this enduring attraction of green for yellow, and vice versa.

I define green and yellow men as natural men, green being the earth man and yellow the sky man. Their erotic bond belongs to nature. There are also red and blue men, cultural men representing the arts and sciences, respectively. They make up the other axis in a typology of male-male relationships. Here, however, we will be concerned with red and blue only as necessary to provide a contrast.

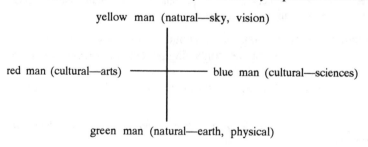

yellow man (natural—sky, vision)

red man (cultural—arts) —————|————— blue man (cultural—sciences)

green man (natural—earth, physical)

[18] *Homosexuality: The Psychology of the Creative Process.*
[19] Herbert Mason, *Gilgamesh: A Verse Narrative*, p. 24.

Some might object to my labeling blue and red men (especially red) as cultural rather than natural. I do recognize the connection of red with blood, the juice of life, and so with the earliest activities of man (such as hunting and many initiation rites), but blood was not the precise aim of these activities; it was one of the accompaniments. The precise aim was survival, which a union of yellow, the man of vision, with green, the physical man, made possible. The exact measured grasp of the environment, which I would call blue, and the capacity to give values to an experience of that environment, which I call red, developed later. In my model of typology, red and blue relate to yellow and green as Jung's feeling and thinking functions relate to intuition and sensation, that is, as rational to irrational. (Some Jungians have used these very colors to delineate the four functions themselves.)

Also inherent in the green-yellow typology are certain Jungian concepts related to male-male interaction such as the dark and light brothers or senex and puer, not to mention Jung's ideas about intuition and sensation. What appeals to me most about the green-yellow typology, though, is the possibilities it holds out for a symbolic and imagistic approach to male homosexual or homoerotic relationships.[20] What it allows me to do is to weave a tapestry around the subject where the hundreds of colored threads, drawn from a wide selection of sources, depict its rough outlines rather than its exquisite details.

One warning is in order. I am, not suprisingly, a yellow man—authors of such works usually are. A green man would doubtless have chosen another medium, perhaps dance or clay or paint, to communicate his perceptions of the yellow-green bond. What follows will therefore demonstrate a greater fascination (complete with blind spots and prejudices) for the green half of the relationship, who, after all, represents the numinous Other for this author.

---

[20] This typology could be applied to the dynamics operating in certain male-female relationships. It is not, however, generally applicable as it is in male-male relationships. For example, the myth of Apollo, the Greek sun-god, and the nymph Daphne, who was turned into a laurel tree, might be construed as yellow-green, as might that of Apollo and Cyrene, the Thessalian shepherdess; but that of Apollo with Cassandra, the doomed seeress of Troy, or of Apollo with Coronis, mother of Asclepius, god of healing, cannot. In Northern mythology, we might find yellow and green working in the attraction of Brünnhilde to Siegfried; we don't find it in Elsa's relationship to Lohengrin. And, in Biblical mythology, can we interpret the relationship of Samson and Delilah or Ruth and Boaz or Esther and Ahasuerus as green-yellow? I think not. With male-male relationships, regardless of culture and epoch, green and yellow, appearing in one of the two configurations described above, are inevitably present. All of Apollo's erotic relationships with men are of the yellow-green sort.

How this model applies to female-female relationships, if at all, I must leave to others.

2
Green Men and Yellow Men

The Green Man

When I was in high school, no boy would dare to wear green on Thursday for fear of being called a "mo" (homosexual); it was the very last accusation a suburban Canadian schoolboy of the mid-sixties wanted to support.

The linking of Thursday with so-called homosexual behavior was, at least, a witty one—although accusers and accused were unlikely to have been aware of that—since the god Thor, after whom the day is named, won back the hammer of the gods from the frost giants by posing *en travesti* as a prospective bride of the thief. (Loki was naturally in attendance as maid-in-waiting.) In Latin countries, too, Thurs-day—*jeudi, giovedi, joi,* etc.—is also named after a god (Jupiter, Jove) who is associated with homosexual activity, albeit more explicitly, in the rape of Ganymede. But what signified the coupling of green with homosexuality? What brought these two together?

In the 1890s, green was one of two colors most commonly associated with the Aesthetic Movement, the movement of dandies and decadent artists among whom green was valued for what Alfred Ziegler would call its "morbistic" qualities. Holbrook Jackson wrote in 1913: "It was fashionable in 'artistic' circles [of the 1890s] to drink absinthe and to discuss its 'cloudy green' suggestiveness."[21] That *fin-de-siècle* dandy and man-of-letters Richard Le Gallienne commented thus on green's popularity:

> There is something not quite good, something almost sinister, about it—at least, in its more complex forms, though in its simple form, as we find it in outdoor nature, it is innocent enough; and, indeed, is it not used in colloquial metaphor as an adjective for innocence itself? . . . But Becky Sharp's eyes also were green, and the green of the aesthete does not suggest innocence.[22]

It was just this something sinister, this lack of innocence that the badge—or one of the badges—of the Aesthetic Movement, the green carnation, expressed by its very unnaturalness.

We might be justified in looking for a connection between the Canadian schoolboys' accusation and the 1890s' preference for green—Oscar Wilde was, after all, the chief spokesman of *fin-de-siècle* aestheticism—but as Le Gallienne

---

[21] *The Eighteen Nineties,* p. 153.
[22] Ibid., p. 169.

himself pointed out, green is most often associated with the very opposite of sinister. At least it is as much the color of life, of healthy, glowing life as it is of life diseased, rotting or poisoned, life mangled by such emotions as envy. For most of us, green means the inexorable cycles of Mother Nature—birth, growth, decay, rebirth, enacted in forests, meadows, hills and dales, not in opium-scented drawing rooms.

Green is the innocence of undiluted nature. Jung, in his alchemical writings, refers often to the "benedicta viriditas" or blessed greenness which he defines as "life in the chthonic sense,"[23] and in other places as the future. From the *Rosarium philosophorum*, he extracts the following paean to green: "O blessed greenness, which gives birth to all things, whence know that no vegetable and no fruit appears in the bud but that it hath a green colour."[24] This blessed greenness, which the twelfth-century German mystic Hildegard of Bingen called "greening power,"[25] was the color of "the spontaneous perfect harmony of humans in nature."[26] Hildegard and alchemists of a later date credited the Holy Ghost with responsibility for the earth's bountiful greenness. However, this was but a Christianization of a very old archetype, which John Michell has named the earth spirit. In the age of Cronus, Michell tells us,

> [men] were ruled not by other men but by spirits, these corresponding to the eternal element in nature. [They] were wanderers, living under the direct guidance and protection of the earth spirit, following the migratory paths of their ancestors, vitally concerned with the cycles of the animal and plant life, the progress of the seasons, the movements of the heavenly bodies.[27]

Rocks, trees, mountains, wells and springs were receptacles for that spirit. Later legends of a King of the Forest who lives in a hut under the earth where everything, including the people, is green reflect the same idea: a vegetation or tree numen, the spirit of green growing. By the time the alchemists were seeking to release spirit from matter (as if spirit did not belong there as well as in the Christian Heaven!), the world of the earth spirit had long ago succumbed to the pressure of the solar deities and given over its shrines to their use. Apollo's defeat of the telluric serpent who reigned at Delphi before him is perhaps the most famous example of such a surrender. Michell speaks of the "crime of settlement,"[28] and the beginnings of the exploitation of earth marked by a "policy of

---

[23] "A Study in the Process of Individuation," *The Archetypes and the Collective Unconscious,* CW 9i, par. 566.

[24] *Aion,* CW 9ii, par. 386n.

[25] *Illuminations of Hildegard of Bingen,* p. 113.

[26] Ibid., p. 112.

[27] *The Earth Spirit: Its Ways, Shrines and Mysteries,* p. 3.

[28] Ibid., p. 8.

artificially increasing the earth's fertility and multiplying the gifts of its spirit, instead of accepting what is given by nature."[29] This policy, which has led to a wholesale destruction of nature, demonstrates a nearly hysterical fear and loathing on the part of patriarchal authority for the awesome—but not unbreakable—powers of the old matriarchal regime.

We must not forget that this green world belonged once to the Great Mother, Magna Mater, in both her beneficent and terrifying aspects. Inanna, Ishtar, Demeter, Isis and Ceres were but some of her names. Nature and Earth are, in fact, still called Mother, especially by those who live close to her and depend on her bounty for their survival. There is no need here to expand on the connection between nature and the maternal feminine—it is as old as the oldest creation myths. I do not subscribe to an exclusively feminine definition of the earth mysteries—some participation by a chthonic, phallic power was crucial to their performance[30]—but neither do I deny the overriding importance of the part played by the feminine. This power of the maternal feminine may be the same that lies behind the sixties' scorn for schoolboys caught wearing green on Thursday.

A man or boy who wears green proclaims his closeness not just to earth but also to mother and her nurturing world. He is a "Mama's boy," a "sissy," concepts that have traditionally led to suspicions of homosexuality. As many contemporary psychologists will attest, however, Mama's boys are not necessarily budding homosexuals; they are at least as frequently found among heterosexual men.[31] By wearing green, a man or boy also demonstrates his familiarity with the body and its feelings or sensations, just those areas of the maternal world that a patriarchal Judeo-Christian ethos has made such a profound source of embarrassment and ridicule.

The green man I wish to discuss is, in fact, a Mama's boy, at least in the sense that he lives close to Mother Nature, works in her name and honors her, acknowledging her sacredness. He is the son analytical psychology has long mourned in Tammuz who was, as M. Esther Harding reminds us,[32] Urkittu or the Green One; or in his counterparts, Osiris, Attis and Adonis—the son sacrificed to his mother's lust, the typical son-hero who never rises to the challenges posed by consciousness which the true hero invariably meets with great success.

---

[29] Ibid., p. 19.

[30] See Eugene Monick, *Phallos: Sacred Image of the Masculine.*

[31] Jung believed that a man with a mother complex was just as likely to become a Don Juan. ("Psychological Aspects of the Mother Complex," *The Archetypes and the Collective Unconscious,* CW 9i, par. 162) Monick suggests a simple formula: "If a man is in need of more father, he is homosexual; if a man is in need of more mother, he is heterosexual; if a man is in need of more of both, he is bisexual." (*Phallos,* p. 120)

[32] *Woman's Mysteries, Ancient and Modern,* chapter 12.

But Tammuz, Attis and the other vegetation or fertility gods who every year suffer death and resurrection are only one face of the green man and, most importantly, not the homosexual face that concerns us here.[33]

The Flower Boy

The green man has many faces. Goethe described how the maturing of green is a darkening process:

> We have seen . . . that the germ pushing from the earth is generally white and yellowish, but by the means of the action of light and air it acquires a green colour. The same happens with young leaves of trees, as may be seen, for example, in the birch, the young leaves of which are yellowish, and, if boiled, yield a beautiful yellow juice: afterwards they become greener, while the leaves of other trees become gradually blue-green.[34]

This yellowish-green describes the type of green man I call the Flower Boy.

Yellow-green we normally associate with the spring, with what is new, hopeful, *in potentia,* and so belongs to youth in all its innocence and freshness. "Green as grass! a regular cabbage head" is how such a youth (obviously a Dummling) is described by Herman Melville.[35] Thomas Mann compares his head to a flower poised above his collar "in incomparable loveliness. It was the head of Eros, with the yellowish bloom of Parian marble."[36] Fragile is this type as youth itself is fragile, fleeting.

In Greek mythology, we find several examples of the yellowish, spring-green man or flower boy. Hyacinthus, beloved of Apollo, is one. Let Ovid tell his story.

> One day, near noon . . .
> They both stripped off their clothes and oiled their limbs,
> So sleek and splendid, and began the game,
> Throwing the discus; and Apollo first
> Poised, swung and hurled it skywards through the air,
> Up, soaring up, to cleave the waiting clouds.
> The heavy disk at longest last fell back
> To the familiar earth, a proof of skill,
> And strength with skill. Then straightway Hyacinth,
> Unthinking, in the excitement of the sport,
> Ran out to seize it, but it bounded back

---

[33] Bernard Sergent looks at the relationship between these son-heroes and their homosexual counterparts in *Homosexuality in Greek Myths*. There, he stoutly refutes the agrarian character of the rites and festivals held in honor of the latter. I refer the interested reader to part 3, chapter 8 of Sergent's book.

[34] *Theory of Colours,* pp. 50-51.

[35] *Redburn,* p. 75.

[36] *Death in Venice and Seven Other Stories,* p. 29.

Caravaggio, *Boy with Fruit Basket*
(Borghese Gallery, Rome)

From the hard surface full into his face.
The god turned pale, pale as the boy himself,
And catching up the huddled body, tried
To revive him, tried to staunch the tragic wound
And stay the fading soul with healing herbs.
His skill was vain; the wound was past all cure.
And as, when in a garden violets
Or lilies tawny-tongued or poppies proud
Are bruised and bent, at once they hang their heads
And, drooping, cannot stand erect and bow
Their gaze upon the ground; so dying lies
That face so fair and, all strength ebbed away,
His head, too heavy, on his shoulder sinks.[37]

Narcissus is another. In the original version of the myth, Sergent explains, Narcissus is a very handsome young man who spurns the love of another young man named Ameinias.

One day he even sends him an ironic gift: a sword. Ameinias then takes this sword and stabs himself in front of Narcissus's house, cursing his beloved as he dies. Shortly thereafter, Narcissus sees his reflection in a well and falls in love with himself. This unbearable contradiction is the cause of his suicide.[38]

From the blood of the dying Narcissus grows, of course, the flower of the same name.

Still another celebrated flower boy from the Greco-Roman world is Cyparissus. He, too, was beloved of Apollo, and so saddened by the loss of his favorite stag whose "antlers gleamed with gold"[39] that he begged his lover to allow him to mourn forever.

. . . And now, with endless sobs,
With lifeblood drained away, his limbs began
To take a greenish hue; his hair that curled
Down from his snowy brow rose in a crest,
A crest of bristles, and as stiffness spread
A graceful spire gazed at the starry sky.[40]

Cyparissus became the cypress tree, familiar of graveyards and burial rites.

We meet later examples of such boys in the sonnets of Shakespeare, the love poems of the so-called Uranians as well as the elegies of the Great War poets—fleeting, fragile youth whose death, like that of Hyacinthus, has a special mean-

---

[37] *Metamorphoses,* book 10, pp. 230-231. (See illustration below, p. 54)
[38] *Homosexuality in Greek Myth,* p. 82.
[39] *Metamorphoses,* book 10, p. 228.
[40] Ibid., p. 229.

ing divorced from the agrarian rituals that claimed the life of Tammuz and his ilk. We shall return to this subject and to the significance of the flower, fruit or tree that comes to represent the lost youth.

The French homeopath Léon Vannier, in his elaborate typology based on classical myth, places our flower boy under the heading, "Hebe," who was a female counterpart to Ganymede in Jove's court. Hebe, Vannier claims, is composed of elements of Saturn, Apollo and the Moon. With contributions from such formidable divinities, we are surprised to find the Hebe type described only as "a type of ephebe [late teen-ager], feminine and narcissistic."[41] He possesses "a beautiful, lithe body, but without soul. Dominant faculty: indifference. Moral sickness: narcissism."[42] Hyacinthus as a variation on the type has at least Marsian influences added to those of Hebe.

Vannier describes one face of the flower-boy type of green man. The narrator of a Romanian novel, speaking of his charmed boyhood, describes another:

Being hot-house flowers . . . brought up in an atmosphere of perfume and cushions, we only knew the joys of our mother's boudoir: dancing, singing, flirting and eating. All that was delicious,[43]

The flower boy is frequently found in such settings, in aristocratic salons, scented bedchambers and the heated imaginations of the Decadents. He is nearly always too beautiful, too delicate, even fey. He exudes an air—albeit gently—of tragedy. Sickness and misfortune lurk about him like rapacious animals.

He was white and delicate as sawn ivory, and his curls were like the rings of the daffodil. His lips, also, were like the petals of a red flower, and his eyes were like violets by a river of pure water, and his body like the narcissus of a field where the mower comes not.
Yet did his beauty work him evil.[44]

Two centuries earlier, Saikaku Ihara offered his impressions of a flower boy:

Passing by a little waterfall in the temple garden, he saw a beautiful young man. This youth was wearing a large hat decorated with silk and kept in place by a pale blue ribbon: his wide-sleeved robe was as purple as the glory of morning flowers: he carried at his girdle two swords in wonderfully-ornamented scabbards: he was walking at ease carrying a branch of yellow flowers in his hand. His beauty was such that Guzayemon for a moment asked himself if the god Roya had not taken human form, or if a peony had not come to life and was walking in the spring sunlight.[45]

---

41 *La typologie et ses applications thérapeutiques,* p. 245. [Author's translation]
42 Ibid., p. 246.
43 Panait Istrati, *Kyra Kyralina,* p. 109.
44 Oscar Wilde, *The Star-Child,* in *Complete Shorter Fiction,* pp. 240-241.
45 *Comrade Loves of the Samurai,* pp. 53-54.

Such a boy can lead a samurai to become a beggar for love, as Guzayemon's fate shows. Indeed, Vannier's "narcissistic ephebe" is exactly the type who lures a man to perdition. In Mann's *Death in Venice*, Tadzio, whom Aschenbach compares to both Narcissus and Hyacinthus, reveals a fragility that is somehow sinister and corrupt, itself carrying whiffs of the dreaded plague. Erick von Lhomond's impressions of his lover Conrad, in Marguerite Yourcenar's *Coup de Grâce* (1939), also focus on the corrupt aspects of the flower boy:

> Natures like Conrad's are frail, so they feel at their best when clad in armour. But, turned loose in the world of society or of business, lionized by women or a prey to easy success, they are subject to certain insidious dissolution, like the loathsome decay of iris; those sombre flowers, which, though nobly shaped like a lance, die miserably in their own sticky secretion, in marked contrast to the slow, heroic drying of the rose.[46]

Sometimes this fragility can show itself fearless or shameless in its defiance or indifference. For instance, with Genet's handsome criminals, like Yeux-Verts (Green Eyes!) who commits murder with a cluster of lilacs between his teeth and in his hair, or Maurice who imagines an apotheosis as a rose, the risks are at least clear; their allure is a dare. With Irene Handl's Benoît, the tragic rich boy whose voice is "harsh like the voice of an exotic bird, and his violet-black hair" like "plumage,"[47] bravado leads to the ultimate dare: suicide.

Vannier's view is too narrow and too negative, however, for the flower boy's fragility is often offset by a playfulness that we generally know as "animal spirits." Spring, after all, is an invigorating time of year, associated with health and innocence. So von Lhomond also records Conrad's "dare-devil courage which he used to display when, like someone moving in a trance, he would leap onto the back of a bull, or of a surging wave";[48] for a moment we almost forget "a small scar on his lip, like a dark violet."[49]

Similarly, the hero of Wilde's fairy tale, *The Young King*, is "wild-eyed and open-mouthed, like a brown woodland Faun, or some young animal of the forest newly snared by the hunters."[50] A little later, we hear of "a bright lustre [in] his dark woodland eyes" as well as of the pale poppies embroidered on the silk coverlet of his bed and of "a laughing Narcissus in green bronze [who] held a polished mirror above its head."[51] With Wilde's Faun sprawled on his royal bed of poppies go many a companion, including the young shepherds of Virgil (especially

---

[46] *Coup de Grâce*, p. 96.
[47] *The Gold Tip Pfitzer*, p. 143.
[48] *Coup de Grâce*, p. 27.
[49] Ibid.
[50] *Complete Shorter Fiction*, p. 171.
[51] Ibid., p. 174.

the cruel Alexis of the second *Eclogue)* and Housman's "light-foot" Shropshire lads.[52]

In both modes, youthful beauty, the beauty of youth is what the flower boy radiates. Nothing sinister or corrupt in that. It is a beauty that has inspired not only poets but also painters and sculptors, particularly in eras when homoeroticism was freely countenanced. The artistic products of ancient Greece, the Renaissance, the *fin-de-siècle* are enamored of his image. The paintings of Henry Scott Tuke (1858-1929), to name but one prolific worshiper of the flower boy's beauty, lovingly depict adolescent youth playing in the light and water of southwest coast England. Such paintings proclaim not only the magic of youthful beauty but through it the magic of Nature herself. "Many of his [Tuke's] ideas were based on the pantheistic belief that god was present in nature, and it was the beauty of nature he worshipped."[53]

This then is the flower-boy type of green man. Before we leave him we should probably say a word about his relation to the puer aeternus or eternal child. First of all, they are not the same. The puer is green only in the sense of immaturity, otherwise he eschews all association with it. Green means *mater* in its several senses and this is precisely not the puer's strong point; he shuns earthy commitment, earthy reality, preferring to escape into the wide open spaces of his imagination but, in so doing, he "has life for an enemy."[54] Thus, he approaches more closely to the realm of the yellow man. The puer's color is that of James Hillman's "primordial golden shadow . . . our angelic essence as messenger of the divine."[55] He resembles nothing so much as the shimmering Lucifer who appears in Matthew Gregory Lewis's Gothic novel, *The Monk,* or in Béjart's ballet-spectacle, *Notre Faust.* He is the classical ballet dancer par excellence, encouraged away from his roots, his standpoint in reality, by the inorganic discipline of the Sun King's Academy.

Hillman, nonetheless, attempts to saddle Hyacinthus and his peers with the label of puer—puer felled by negative senex[56]—but I feel he thus misleads us. Hyacinthus and company are not high-flying boys. Their essential quality is their earthboundedness, their corruptibility. Puers are incorruptible, that's what makes them "aeternus" after all. Their bodies are only appendages to their glowing fantasy life, whereas the reverse is true for flower boys.

Ganymede might wear the puer label better; to be the eternal companion and cupbearer of the King of Heaven is a fantasy many a puer might confess to.

---

[52] *A Shropshire Lad,* p. 83.

[53] Emmanuel Cooper, *The Life and Work of Henry Scott Tuke, 1858-1929,* p. 41.

[54] Jung, *Symbols of Transformation,* CW 5, par. 615.

[55] *Puer Papers,* p. 26.

[56] Ibid., p. 27.

Icarus, too, another beautiful ephebe (if, that is, we can believe Draper's famous portrait of him lamented by nymphs that hangs in the Tate Gallery) could stand as a model for puer psychology. He has long been a popular subject for sculptors—Alfred Gilbert's *Icarus* of 1884, for example—and ballet choreographers. One of the latter, Gerald Arpino, suggested an intensely erotic tie between Icarus and his father, Daedalus, in a ballet called *The Relativity of Icarus* (1974). If we accept Arpino's view, then we must be prepared to see Dædalus as the green one, and no flower boy either.

Let me conclude this section by saying that the flower-boy type of green man, the spring-green man, represents most often a phase, not a final position. He gives no promise of developing into a fully fledged green man; he could as easily lead to red, blue or yellow developments as to green. Spring green conceals a rainbow of possibilities which make it difficult to define. Many men pass through this phase and most never look back. But there are those who do, those who linger, and for their sake and in honor of their longing, this type of green, so fragile, so little-tried, must take its proper place in our gallery of green men.

The Gardener

Léon Vannier has given us a description of the second of our green types, the most familiar and populous category of green, which in terms of its maturity or darkness, I would call summer green. This is the deep, rich green of the forest in August, Lincoln green, Robin Hood green, the green of Sir Frederick Ashton's balletic Oberon. I name this type the Gardener. Vannier calls him simply Earth-man. He has a "face the shape of a chestnut,"[57] notes Vannier, and "a heavy, ponderous bearing."[58] He continues:

> Their great superiority resides in the rectitude of their judgment, in their common sense, which allows them to manage their lives well. They have an innate sense of justice and balance.[59]

Intellectually, "they comport themselves like true ruminants":

> In the sciences, they lean on facts, on experience. In the arts, they are the realists, the naturalists. Their artistic abilities are not, in fact, very remarkable. What they look for above all is the solid, decent and well-made.[60]

Moreover, Vannier insists, "the Earth-man," besides being sedentary, attached to hearth, home and country,

---

[57] *La typologie,* p. 218.
[58] Ibid., p. 219.
[59] Ibid., p. 221.
[60] Ibid.

is always at bottom a peasant. He loves country life and its occupations. Whatever his social situation might be, he surrenders willingly to the cares of the garden and he never feels himself to be stooping when wielding a shovel or rake.[61]

In the Lüscher color test, the green, a trifle bluer than our summer green should be, nevertheless echoes some of Vannier's observations, expressing firmness, constancy, resistance to change and pride of possessions. Green here corresponds to "the majestic sequoia, deep-rooted, proud and unchanging, towering over lesser trees."[62] Among its other qualities, according to Lüscher, are persistence, self-assertion, obstinacy, defensiveness, retentiveness. To these, Annie Wilson and Lilla Bek make the following additions:

> Green people are aware of nature and have an affinity with plants. They make good gardeners and farmers . . . Green people enjoy children . . . and animals. A green person hates pollution and because he ranges into the blue ray he is drawn to water, lakes and sea. He is temperamentally more balanced than other colours and less easily offended because he makes excuses for people.[63]

However, his soft heart makes the gardener very vulnerable and he is easily taken advantage of.

The soft heart belongs to the gardener because green is the color of the heart chakra, the Anahata lotus, the place of the unstruck sound where the Yogi says God reaches down to man. The cardiac area, green country, is the source, explains Arnold Mindell, of those functional problems medicine has named hypochondria: "The unconscious reaches down into conscious life and may be heard and controlled in this area through the breath."[64]

Astrology locates the gardener type in the earth signs, particularly, I would say, in Taurus, the Bull. A young analysand, himself an astrologer born in the sign of Taurus, speaks often of his Taurean need for a fixed point, his stubbornness, his sensuality. He once told me that a Taurus man loves to lie or roll in the grass, feel the earth between his fingers, smell the scents of the land. A Taurus farmer, if he were true to himself, would never buy a tractor "because it stinks and makes a noise"; he would prefer "a simple plough."

Many attempts have been made to define the green man we have called the gardener (for most people, there exists no other type), but I think we have heard enough to get a sense of him. Perhaps I would add only one further observation; namely, that Jung's sensation type, whether the concrete (sensuous) or abstract

---

[61] Ibid., p. 223.
[62] Ian A. Scott, *The Lüscher Color Test*, p. 67.
[63] *What Colour are You?*, p. 25.
[64] *Dream Body: The Body's Role in Revealing the Self*, p. 42.

variety, has several things in common with our gardener type, a finely honed sense of reality chief among them. To summarize, I offer the following portrait.

The gardener is a man of any age. He gives an impression of physical strength even when he is slight or willowy. In fact, his "body self" is always very present without ever being self-conscious. He is not embarrassed by any physical act; he is at home in the physical realm. His character tends to be slow, dreamy (in the sense of unambitious), steady, reliable, predictable, obstinate. He is generally a man of few words, gives the appearance of passivity and of going with the flow, so that he often earns accusations of stupidity or oafishness—and he can be, of course—but he, all the same, knows very well where his limits are, knows where he stands, as anyone who tries to push him too far will attest. His anger, though not easily roused, is ferocious. Otherwise, he is attentive, easy-going, open to suggestion, precisely because his roots are down.

These roots do not, as some complain, prevent him from playing—for the gardener loves to play as much as any child, whether engaging in games or pranks or rolling in the grass; rather, they give his *joie de vivre* a deeper resonance. Sentimentality colors his affective expression which generally has a warm, nurturing, even motherly quality. He likes to provide for others, especially food, physical comforts, sex. He can use these, in fact, as mother does, to possess the recipient. He is very possessive. In its shadow manifestations, his sexuality is that of the hedonist, the Epicurean, the sybarite. Even within a monogamous relationship, he knows no sexual inhibition, and yet, what Vannier has called "an innate sense of justice and balance"[65] comes into play whenever sexuality—or anything else—threatens to overrun his life. For the gardener is basically a conservative soul. Combined with obstinacy and reluctance to change, this can, of course, lead to an unyielding dogmatism, a sticking to the law that strikes a fascist note. The dictator is a familiar unconscious figure to gardener types who follow their dreams and their fantasies.

Ancestors of the gardener type of green man are the fertility and vegetation gods of the ancient world. The cabiri, homunculi and other little men, like the Irish leprechaun, who are the Great Mother's attendants, belong also to his family tree. Other branches contain the many suckling giants of Grimm and the trolls of Scandinavian mythology, as well as animals like the fox, frog and snake who help the hero on his journey through fairy tale country. These figures are not just stooges of the Great Mother. They know her secrets, guard her treasures, yes, but they are also powerful chthonic forces in their own right, if not by virtue of their brute strength then by their mercurial wiliness. To this band belongs Mercurius himself *(Mercurius vegetativus)* and other elusive spirits in-

---

[65] *La typologie,* p. 221.

habiting the natural world, fairy folk like Shakespeare's Oberon and Puck or England's famed "Green Man."

Marc Alexander recounts the history of the Green Children of Suffolk, which dates from the reign of King Stephen (twelfth century).[66] They were a brother and a sister who were guarding their flocks one day in the twilight world of St. Martin's Land, where everything and everyone is green, when the ringing of many bells drew them to a cave. They entered and, after exploring it, came out the other side and found themselves in England. The dazzling sunlight blinded them long enough to facilitate their discovery and capture. Surprised by their green appearance, their captors questioned them intensively but the pair could not understand; they spoke a special language. The only food they would accept were beans—in Celtic folklore, the food of the dead. The brother soon died pining for home and the sister, whose color eventually faded to white, was taken on as a servant in a lord's home. It is said she accepted baptism, but nonetheless remained rather wanton and loose, accusations hurled even today at the green man's head.

England's "Green Man," whose face peering out of a fan of branches adorns the signs of many English pubs (one in London's St. Martin's Lane) as well as carved reliefs in many cathedrals, including Norwich and Southwell, is one of those vegetation or tree numens mentioned earlier, sometimes beneficent, sometimes wild and sometimes, like the fairy folk, mischievous.

Dionysus, god of the vine, and that son of Hermes-Mercury, the goat-footed piper Pan, represent yet another branch of the gardener's ancestry, the branch that bequeathed him his sensual appetites and capacity for sexual abandon. Mindell has called Mercury, progenitor of Pan, the god of the body, symbolizing uncontrolled physical energy. "Physiologically, he is found in the body in the form of sexual impulses, compulsions and spontaneous body motions."[67]

A recent trend in analytical psychology has been to view homosexual phenomena as expressions of another son of Hermes-Mercury (though some say, of Dionysus), that is, of Priapus, the gross-genitaled antique god of "male fruitfulness in Nature."[68] Among other things, Priapus was the protector of various forms of agriculture, cattle-breeding, gardens, vineyards, hunters, etc., and so accords well with my account of the gardener type. But neither the gardener nor homosexuality in general can be understood in terms of a monumental priapic erection. To try to do so is also reductionist.[69]

---

[66] *British Folklore,* pp. 98-99.

[67] *Dream Body,* p. 59.

[68] Ad de Vries, *Dictionary of Symbols and Imagery,* p. 373.

[69] The symbolic significance of Priapus is explored at length in James Wyly, *The Phallic Quest: Priapus and Masculine Inflation.*

Above: Paul Cadmus, *The Cecropia Helmet,* 1972
Below: Norwich Cathedral, *Green Man,* 14th cent.

Our gardener's more human relations are, of course, the antique shepherds of Virgil or Spenser, or the modern ones of Housman; the woodsmen of Robin Hood legends or of Grimm; and the farmers, gardeners, gamekeepers and country bumpkins of Western European and, especially, English fiction right up to the First World War. (Is Triptolemus the "genius" presiding over all such figures? He was, remember, the young man to whom Demeter, the nature goddess, bequeathed the secrets of agriculture so that he might teach them to mankind.) The agricultural professions remain attractive to contemporary gardener types. Other professions where we find him today—florist, chef, healthcare worker, masseur—are only refinements of that concern for "natural" phenomena demonstrated by the more rustic occupations.

The rustic or pastoral setting is the traditional one for our hero. Even today the dreams of modern men stress its symbolic appropriateness for the kind of discovery the green part in us is best able to undertake, the discovery of our real "nature." An analysand who is, I think, a gardener type, but embarrassed to express it and so remains a rather frustrated flower boy at twenty five, often dreams of his younger brother, who is by profession a gardener, in lush settings:

> I am gathering flowers with Claude [his brother] in a large meadow. I am carrying the flowers, though the bouquet we are creating is his. I remark on the different kinds of flowers. Only scabiosa is missing. I add to the bouquet hydrangea which are moist and, I remark, rotten. Then comes a telephone call from my mother who wants us to make another fresh bouquet for her.

Some time later, he dreamed:

> I go through a flower meadow on the side of a hill, singing. I see a pair of lovers who have a kind of quarrel. I wonder whether I should stop singing, but then I think of "Reto" [his lover] and so I continue. I then come to a large meadow where the flowers come up to my chin.

Such images compensate in part for the repression of the dreamer's desire to work with flowers, which pressure to win academic honors for the family demands of him, he believes. The lushness of the setting to which, in the second dream, the male lover gives his support stands in direct opposition to the limitations imposed on the analysand's life through the family's expectations, expressed directly (mother's telephone call) and indirectly (the question, "Should I go on singing?").

The spring-green man, or flower boy, showed himself the mother's son, first chronologically, that is, all young men are closer to mother and the matriarchal realm than are old men; and second, by acting as the representative of one of her most pleasurable phases, beguiling youth. But the summer-green man, or gardener, represents the destructive as well as the pleasurable aspects of the Great Mother. He supports life in its raw, organic form; celebrates it, in fact, as we have seen. Life, however, is part of a cycle that includes death, too. This green man is not afraid of death. While the flower-boy type is often caught unawares by death, like Hyacinthus by the discus or Conrad by a bullet, the gardener expects death, plays with it, sometimes even seeks it.

E.M. Forster, a novelist fascinated by the effects of green men on polite society, observed of the green hero of his short story *The Purple Envelope:* "And Howard loved to take life, as all those do who are really in touch with nature."[70] A similar observation is made about his gamekeeper Scudder, beloved by the eponymous hero of *Maurice* (1913): "He liked the woods and the fresh air and water, he liked them better than anything and he liked to protect or destroy life."[71]

In another of Forster's stories, the eerie *Dr. Woolacott,* the attractive, smiling and nameless stranger, "fresh as a daisy, strong as a horse,"[72] turns out, in fact, to be a chimera, a psychopomp leading the invalided hero out of the clutches of the butcher-doctor of the title into the land of the dead:

> They entwined more closely, their lips touched never to part, and then something gashed him where life had concentrated, and Dr Woolacott, arriving too late, found him dead on the floor.[73]

But it's not just Forster's fantasy. In Julien Green's 1953 play about the antebellum south of America called *Sud* (South), the dark, handsome, earnest and unconsciously homosexual plantation owner, Erik MacClure, is a green man-gardener as angel-of-death, administering the fatal blow to the man who loves him and justifying it as a natural phenomenon.

The beautiful sculpture by Hamo Thornycroft, *The Mower* (above, page 6), a copy of which is housed in London's Tate Gallery, depicts the same type caught as it were in a pause from work. His figure was inspired in part by a Matthew Arnold poem, *Thyrsis:*

> A Mower, who, as a tiny swell
> Of our boat passing heaved the river grass,
> Stood with suspended scythe to see us pass.[74]

At first glance, this mower is just a fine specimen of the English country worker whose physical splendor pays tribute to the Great Goddess he serves, but when we take into consideration the symbolism of his scythe (not to mention the prominence of the word "pass" in the poem that led to his creation), then he

---

[70] *The Life to Come and Other Stories,* p. 54.

[71] *Maurice,* p. 192.

[72] *The Life to Come and Other Stories,* p. 117.

[73] Ibid., pp. 126-127.

[74] Benedict Read, *Victorian Sculpture,* p. 326.

becomes as well a kind of athletic grim reaper. The scythe in Thornycroft's sculpture also reminds us that it is used to tame or contain the bounty of nature and that our gardener type is no more Nature's vassal than were his archaic counterparts. His consciousness is colored by her rhythms and moods, but he is no less conscious for that. He can indeed develop a very deep and resonating wisdom. This belongs to the third and last category of green man, but before we leave the second, here is a portrait of him by the Irish writer Forrest Reid (1875-1947), who specialized in chronicles of boyhood.

In *Uncle Stephen,* the young hero, Tom Barber, flees his unsympathetic stepfamily and goes in search of his unknown blood relative, the uncle of the title. As he approaches the mysterious domain of this most mysterious relative, he encounters not a soul, then

> he drew near the bridge, where a young man stood facing him, with his right arm stretched along the parapet. . . . The attitude of the loiterer was graceful and indolent, he might have been standing for his portrait, yet somehow at that first glance, Tom had received a faintly disquieting impression, which the dark eyes fixed on him intently did nothing to remove. He thought of gipsies, for this young man, in his rough homespun jacket and leather leggings, did not look like a farm labourer, though he might have been a gamekeeper; but his deeply tanned complexion and the scarlet neckcloth he wore loosely knotted round his muscular throat were very much in keeping with Tom's conception of a gipsy. . . .
>
> And all this time he continued to advance, though with a growing embarrassment. For the young man's stare was persistent, and Tom could not escape from it, even though he kept his own gaze averted. Nor did he altogether like the brown surly face upon which short black hairs showed a weekly shave to be nearly due. There was something in its expression to which he was unaccustomed—something boldly investigatory, vaguely predatory. He himself kept his eyes fixed on the landscape, nor was it till he was actually abreast of the figure leaning against the parapet that the latter spoke. "Evening!" he said.[75]

This green man, gardener type, turns out to be the son of his uncle's housekeeper and the sparkling Tom, very much a yellow man in the making, learns to love him.

The Prophet of the Land

The third category of green man I might simply call the dark green man. He is the color of leaves as they blend into the earth in autumn, of the earth itself hibernating below snow and ice through the winter—a black- or mulch-green. Color theorists refer properly to this as a blue-green that at its bluest, according

---

[75] *Uncle Stephen,* p. 40.

to Scott in *The Lüscher Color Test,* represents a union with Gaea, the Earth Mother. Artistically, however, I feel that black-green is a more appropriate way of denoting this type, whose goal may be better described as a *re*-union with Gaea.

Traditionally, he is an older man, the village sage or wise man of the forest whom the hapless fairy-tale hero often fortuitously encounters and thereby saves himself untold trouble. An analysand dreamt recently of just such a man keeping watch at the mouth of a cave in the forest. If the flower boy and gardener are her sons, then this older man is clearly the bridegroom of the Great Mother. Although their wisdom contains savagery or violence, Iron Hans and Gawain's Green Knight are wise "old" men in this same dark green mould. But he does not have to be old, as we will see. He has only to have a deep and penetrating vision. It is a green where the spiritual side predominates. The flower boy and gardener types may be numinous but their calling is not explicitly a spiritual one. Here, with dark green, it is.

Western culture has rarely allowed green to be spiritual. Green is material after all; it cannot be spiritual, too. Other cultures and other ways, however, disagree. We could cite as one case the Muslim Green Man, El Khidir, who saw through the absurd appearances of the material world to the truths beyond.[76] The patron of travelers and sailors, lord of vegetation as well as of water, El Khidir was, according to some, the son of Adam who rescued his father's corpse from the flood; according to others, the son of Earth herself, growing to manhood on animal milk. With his home at the edge of the world where the two great oceans of heaven and earth touch, he stands as a symbol of the human order midway between high and low. He is variously depicted carrying or seated on a fish or sitting down on white fur which then becomes green. Arab chroniclers identify the green fur as Earth. But what is a heightened feature of this vegetation deity is his deep and wide knowledge. Anyone who meets him must never question him but submit to his counsels no matter how ridiculous they seem—El Khidir knows the way to truth. His services once rendered, he disappears. In this sense, he approaches to those wise old men of Western folklore I mentioned above. And he is, like them, timeless.

The qualities of timelessness and spirituality belong also to the North American Indian's dark green man, whose portrait Walter Williams paints so convincingly in *The Spirit and the Flesh.* He is known by a lot of different names, but the tradition itself which many, if not all, tribes subscribe to Williams calls *berdache.* The word is Persian in origin and describes a young man who plays a passive role in sex with men. The Spanish conquistadors used

---

[76] Jean Chevalier and Alain Gheerbrandt, *Dictionnaire des Symboles,* p. 1003.

a Latinized form of the word to describe the so-called depraved creatures, half men/half women, whom they found among the natives of their New World. What shocked the Spanish (and later explorers) most was that these berdaches were revered as holy men, people with very special powers. The berdache is related to the *kedeshim* or homosexual holy men of the Old Testament purges,[77] and to the *kosio* tradition of the Slave Coast of Africa,[78] among others. It is wrong, however, to imagine the berdache as a phenomenon of gifted youth only; the role demanded a lifetime commitment.

In many tribes, the berdache is the shaman and where he is not he is at least important enough that the shaman would not conduct a ceremony without consulting him. Even in his youth, the berdache is referred to as the wise old man. The processes by which a boy takes up the role of berdache vary from tribe to tribe.[79] One frequently recurring motif is the appearance of the Moon Goddess to the chosen boy in dreams or in the form of visions; she demands his service. His parents recognize her influence on their son by his outer preference for women's activities, women's apparel, women's company. Sometimes his allegiance to the Moon Goddess is tested by ordeals.

North American Indians define weaving, farming, gardening and handicrafts as women's activities (hunting and fishing as men's). Because of his strength— Williams makes very clear that the berdache is morphologically thoroughly masculine—and because his labors are never broken by the demands of pregnancy and child-rearing, he can easily become the tribe's most prolific worker in these fields. He can make himself very rich from his work, too. But material success is only one of the berdache's accomplishments and by no means the most important. As half man, half woman, he plays the role of mediator between the sexes, acting as counselor for marital and other relationship difficulties. To him is often entrusted the education of children and the guardianship of problem adolescents. More important yet is his familiarity with the spirit world; as an interpreter of dreams and visions, he has no peer but the shaman. When he *is* the shaman, he is responsible for the spiritual health of the whole community. It is this inextricable bond of earth and spirit in the life of the berdache that qualifies him as a supreme example of the dark green man, or Prophet of the Land.

In some ways, the berdache resembles Jung's portrait of the man with the positive mother complex.[80] Just as Jung suggested that it is his feminine streak

---

[77] See Tom Horner, *Jonathan Loved David: Homosexuality in Biblical Times,* pp. 59ff.

[78] Edward Carpenter, *Selected Writings,* vol. 1, pp. 258-259.

[79] The tradition, long suppressed in response to white pressure, has in recent years undergone a renaissance.

[80] See above, note 3.

that gives the mother's son his particular sensitivity to relationship, education and the spiritual life, so it is the berdache's heightened relationship to the world of the Great Mother that allows him to render meaningful interpretations of her messages upon which the Indians depend for survival; he is, in fact, a kind of medium through which the earth spirit communicates.[81]

This spirit was the subject of a dream I had of one of my analysands, the Taurean mentioned earlier. I was taking him down into a suite of adobe chambers under the earth; these chambers were full of light.[82] There we joined other Indian warriors to listen to an older, powerfully built Indian wearing a beautiful beaded vest and feathers instruct us in the earth mysteries. He began his lesson with the declaration, "I am the Spirit of the Earth." I am prepared to allow a subjective in-

---

[81] Richard Green's study, *The "Sissy Boy" Syndrome and the Development of Homosexuality,* published only a year before Williams's book, records the labors of over fifteen years' research on so-called effeminate boys. The subjects and their parents were interviewed at intervals over this period to determine what common features their developmental processes might reveal. The wearing of women's clothes in childhood (what the author likes to call "cross-dressing") and a preference for so-called women's activities, imaginative play as opposed to rough-and-tumble, are two such features. One mother, responding to her son's proclivities, admits:

"He is very imaginative in general, very imaginative in his play and he has been since the time he was a little child—from the time he was under two. I was amazed at his ability to pretend and take on roles. This is something he loves to do. He gets great pleasure from this. He is fantastic at accents—at languages. . . . He used to play a lot when he was little, and he usually was the woman. He went through a very brief cowboy stage, and he likes his Indian suit, but for the most part he really takes the role of a girl." (p. 178)

But then she continues in a rather worried way:

"He would wear my shoes, and he would take my purse, and he would say, 'Mommy going to the market.' He had a very special relationship with my mother, and he had an imaginary playmate, and she is a grandmother. He created her with my mother. Anyway, where this was most marked was in nursery school last year, when he was four. He did a tremendous amount of playing house and dressing up. . . . He always dressed like a lady, and whenever I came to get him, I would see him in these elaborate outfits, and my heart would really sink." (Ibid)

The "Sissy Boy" Syndrome is full of such testimony on the part of the parents, but nowhere do they or the author give consideration to the purpose such activity might have. Even when, as in this case, the play-acting seems to have been paving the way for a career in the theater (as director), it does not occur to anyone to ask whether the Moon Goddess (or, at least, Dionysus, god of theater) has been around, as it would the parents of a berdache; there are only endless comparisons of data and Green's final, self-congratulatory (because "liberal"), "We just don't know."

[82] Pueblo Indians, noted for their adobe homes, had a profound respect for the berdache tradition.

terpretation of the dream, for yellow men are often too high up and lack appropriate reverence for this "lower" world and its spirits, a world to be exploited intellectually but not experienced. Objectively speaking though, the dream captures something of my analysand's need as a gardener type to value the "lower" world, not simply as a world of instincts, appetites and regression to mother's womb, but as a spiritual world with its own articles of faith, its own mysteries.

One last image of the prophet of the land, from Western European culture this time, comes from a novella by Jean Giono. The prophet is Elzéard Bouffier, an ageless shepherd whom the author meets in the bleak and lonely hill country of Provence before the First World War. Bouffier shelters Giono, feeds him, lets him silently into his secret. Armed with his iron staff, like the Grimm Brothers' "Young Giant," Bouffier ranges the countryside planting thousands upon thousands of acorns with the belief that trees would bring life back to the land.[83] His belief proves sound and several years later, when the author returns to the region following the war, the land has been transformed; oak trees are growing everywhere, the wilderness is in flower. Such single-minded prophets of the land, such humble fertility gods, echoing like Pan and Dionysus, "the precious secret of humanity's ancient kinship with the earth,"[84] are frequent heroes of Giono's fiction and to them Giono dedicates his art. Norma Goodrich, commenting on Giono's philosophy of art which emphasizes confidence in the future (Bouffier's reforestation program), says,

> Hopefulness must spring, he decided, from literature and the profession of poetry. Authors only write. So, to be fair about it, they have an obligation to profess hopefulness, in return for their right to live and write. The poet must know the magical effect of certain words: hay, grass, meadows, willows, rivers, firs, mountains, hills. . . . The poet's mission is to remind us of beauty, of trees swaying in the breeze, or pines groaning under snow in the mountain passes, of wild white horses galloping across the surf.[85]

Here is perhaps the best description we could ask for, not only of the modern poet's mission, but of the function of green in a despairing society. This green can be of any shade, spring, summer or mulch green; it is in the latter mode, however, that green experience has become wisdom and can be passed on.

All our examples of dark green men are purveyors of wisdom. Our spring-green men, flower boys or *garçons fatals,* are purveyors of youthful beauty and the beauty of youth. Both these types are closer in some ways to the archetypal realm—they are less human. The summer-green type whom we meet most often in the real world often contains something of both extremes: flowerlike beauty

---

[83] Another parallel, more obvious, is the American folk hero, Johnny Appleseed.
[84] *The Man Who Planted Trees,* p. 47.
[85] Ibid., pp. 50-51.

Clare Leighton, *April* (detail)
(from *The Farmer's Year,* 1933)

and dark wisdom. (Just as often though, blue or red auxiliary influences pull him far from his extremes into a more "civilized" comportment.) We might see the extremes as an example of enantiodromia, the flower at the height of its beauty dropping its petals to earth where they become fertilizer for their own reappearance. It is out of the dark, mulch-green that new life "springs" and into it that it returns. We could say that spring green is actually closer to death—its is a doomed loveliness—and dark green to life and eternity even than first appears. The summer-green man is not so often associated with change as with the enduring, perennial face of green, which, yes, knows death, too, but only as another aspect of its enduring quality. Endurance is what counts with him, for otherwise he could not be the helpmate he is for the yellow man, as we will see.

The Green Artist

In our classification so far we have made no mention of the arts as a place where we might find green types. In fact, most of the green men I have known, both through my work and in private life, are involved in the arts, most often as painters, designers, dancers. Green writers are probably few. Harvey, the Egyptologist hero of Susan Hill's *The Bird of Night*, writes treatises on the dynasties, but it is his yellow-man lover, Francis, who is the poet.

I can imagine that Sir Walter Scott's comparison of his own (yellow) work, "the big Bow-Wow strain,"[86] with that of Jane Austen refers to a kind of green writing—"the exquisite touch which renders ordinary commonplace things and characters interesting from the truth of the description and the sentiment."[87] But, can men, whatever their color, manage a touch that is at once homely and exquisite? Nor are we likely to find many green men prominent in the music world, unless they be folk singers or country and western musicians. They may play an instrument or, like the woodland creatures who could not resist Orpheus' lyre, they may be seduced by music, but this is Apollo's domain after all.[88]

Where we are likely to find green men in plenty is, as I've just indicated, in the plastic and performing arts—sculpture, painting, dance—where sensation rules. Objectivity, the value of the object and the universe it contains, is the common concern of green types. Rodin might well have been a green man. So, too, Monet. Novelist Eva Figes offers us an impressionist rendering of Monet's green artistic concerns. We follow the artist on one of his watching and waiting rambles through his grounds; we note with him how the

---

[86] See David Cecil, *A Portrait of Jane Austen*, p. 181.

[87] Ibid.

[88] One must beware of ascribing a green hue to folk music arrangers/collectors such as Canteloube, Percy Grainger, Vaughan Williams, Aaron Copland. These were undoubtedly yellow men fascinated by the green world.

light gleamed on the meadows and pastures beyond, through the same soft white mist, blurring the edges of fence and ditch, bramble, nettle and stunted willow, as the dark night's damp turned back to light and vapour. It clung to the earth's surface, hung above the valley, obscuring the source of light in a soft luminosity, which seemed to come from some dark secret within the earth, rather than the sun, though the two had perhaps colluded.[89]

Later, Figes has Monet exclaim, "We live in a luminous cloud of changing light, a sort of envelope. That is what I have to catch."[90] This is just the image to capture the green man's deepest yearning—a yellow artist would have been straining to catch the earth itself. Vuillard, too, with his densely packed interiors, evoking the homeliness, familiarity, tensions and symbioses of family life ruled by a green-black gowned matriarch at her needle, paints a green man's world. (It was Vuillard who said, "Ma maman, c'est ma Muse!")[91] Like Monet's paintings, they too radiate a light from within.

As for dance, we have already mentioned the appeal it has for the green man. We can point to images of Vaslav Nijinsky in his most famous roles in *Le spectre de la rose* and *L'après-midi d'un faune* as more proof. Or to José Limon, the Hispano-American modern dancer and choreographer whose greatest gift to the dance world besides a series of unforgettable performances (as Judas, the Emperor Jones and the Moor of Venice, to name but three) was a technique based on the laws of gravity called—most fittingly—fall and recovery.

The Yellow Man

We could start our description of the yellow man with accusations like "yellow-bellied" and "jaundice-eyed," but, in fact, they have nothing to do with homosexuality, as wearing green on Thursday does. Granted, Le Gallienne points to the sunflower as the first badge of the aesthetic renaissance of the 1890s. Nor can we forget *The Yellow Book,* one of the bibles of that renaissance, which Holbrook Jackson has described as "newness *in excelsis:* novelty naked and unashamed."[92] Yellow, he continued, "became the colour of the hour, the symbol of the time-spirit. It was associated with all that was bizarre and queer in art and life, with all that was outrageously modern."[93]

But the average person has no knowledge that such a renaissance ever happened, let alone the use it made of the sunflower. Besides, a few outrageous men flaunting—sometimes ironically—the sunflower to demonstrate their aesthetic

---

[89] *Light,* pp. 25-26.

[90] Ibid., p. 78.

[91] Jacques Salomon, *Auprès de Vuillard,* p. 13.

[92] *The Eighteen Nineties,* p. 54.

[93] Ibid.

allegiances could hardly diminish the luster yellow has in our culture.

Above all, yellow signifies sun and light. Since the solar gods first wrested the reins of power from the Magna Mater's grip, yellow has had this meaning. Even today, with the earth reeling from the effects of unfiltered sunlight, the meaning remains for most an unquestionably positive one. There is hardly ever any talk of too much light, only of too little.

Western languages abound with metaphors, figures of speech, clichés expressing the supremacy of yellow values. Indeed, given the sun's position in the sky, above, it's no surprise that yellow is so frequently linked with heights, superiority. Words like illumination and enlightenment automatically evoke images of attainment touching the celestial spheres. Green, by contrast, is "lowly," entirely dependent on the beneficence of the supreme yellow—or, at least, so the solar mythologists have it. I do not want to knock yellow values—enlightenment is one of my aspirations, too—only to pose the question whether in addition to its brilliancy, its commanding position, there are other aspects to yellow.

Jung, who understood solar imagery as a reflection of conscious processes, warned against too one-sided an evaluation of consciousness at the expense of the unconscious.[94] Goethe defined yellow as action, light, brightness, force, warmth, proximity, and then added "repulsion" to the list.[95] "In its highest purity it always . . . has a serene, gay, softly exciting character."[96] It is, on the other hand, "extremely liable to contamination, and produces a very disagreeable effect if it is sullied. . . . Thus, the colour of sulphur, which inclines to green, has a something unpleasant in it."[97]

We can detect from these few remarks, I think, not one yellow, but a whole range from "pure" to "impure"; a happy yellow, warm, carefree, tranquil; a hot, too-hot yellow; a yellow that is maybe a bit aloof (with good reason, for its borders appear to be none too strong); a rancid yellow; a corrosive yellow. As with the Green Man, I am selecting three shades to describe his yellow counterpart: golden yellow, summer sunlight yellow, whitish or moon yellow. Paradoxically —if one takes into account yellow's association with clarity—it is harder to make these three types distinct or clear from one another; there is something insubstantial, elusive, moody, unstable, "liable to contamination" about light, about yellow. You cannot grasp it as you can the earth. Try, and you end up like Forster's Maurice with "arms full of air."[98] Nevertheless, we *will* try.

---

[94] See "The Function of the Unconscious," *Two Essays on Analytical Psychology,* CW 7, par. 275)

[95] *Theory of Colours,* p. 276.

[96] Ibid., p. 307.

[97] Ibid., p. 308.

[98] *Maurice,* p. 144.

The Golden Boy

The maturing of yellow is not a darkening process, as with green, but a lightening one, a move toward the white, not the black. The first of our yellow types, the Golden Boy, is, as his name suggests, the least mature. We discussed him briefly when we looked at the flower boy. He is, as was noted there, Hillman's "primordial golden shadow"[99]—angel, divine messenger, puer. I call him the Golden Boy, even though he is often well past chronological childhood. Earlier I stressed the difference between him and the flower boy. They are drawn to one another though, the beautiful fragility of the one acting as a foil for the beautiful brilliancy of the other. Schoolboy crushes found in novels, films, and sometimes even in life, are frequently composed of such a pair. When the relationship breaks down, the flower boy is always the injured party; he wilts or fades while the golden boy heads for the sky.

The archetype of the divine child lies behind the golden boy. He stands for promise and hopefulness; he is the nascent savior who will redeem the world by innocence, charm, a brilliant flow of ideas and high ideals. Consciously, he defines his task as a reconciliation of the warring opposites and a restoration of balance, harmony. Very often, he gets carried away by this task and forfeits his humanity. In fairy tales, he may appear as a golden child who brings new life, new potential, to a barren or stagnant collective situation. This is his function in Grimm's "Iron Hans" and "The Gold Children." His gold nature also endows him with a fearlessness and a capacity to endure the most horrific experiences as, for example, do the twin heroes of a lovely Romanian tale, "The Boys with the Golden Stars." Princes of the blood, they are buried alive as infants by a scheming queen who wants to steal their birthright; they grow into trees, are cut down and made into beds, are burned, become sparks, which change into fish on touching water, and are then rescued by a fisherman whose attentiveness allows them to resume their human, or rather, superhuman forms, two shining lads with golden stars in the middle of their foreheads. One might say of them, "Too good for this world."

One could certainly say it of Galahad, who also belongs to this group. Of all of the Knights of the Round Table, Galahad remains a golden boy throughout his adventures. He achieves where the others fail and yet he engenders none of the sympathy in us that a Parsifal or Lancelot or even Gawain do, who suffer and in doing so acquire another dimension that fleshes out their youthful idealism. Galahad never swerves, he keeps his eye fixed on Heaven, he is lost to the Spirit. At the same time, his hardiness becomes hardness and inaccessibility. Galahad was a favorite subject of prudish and chauvinistic neo-chivalric romances

---

[99] See above, note 55.

and paintings in Victorian and Edwardian England and he became a point of reference for several chroniclers of the Great War. Through graphic accounts of the death of the beautiful blond male virgin (Galahad was reputedly all of these), his body violated by bullet and bayonet, the devastation of the campaigns on the Western Front gained an added poignancy, not to mention providing a perverse frisson of homoeroticism.

Street Lavendar, Chris Hunt's sentimental, picaresque novel of the life and times of a Victorian hustler, brings the flower-boy hero, Willie, together with a dazzling young aristocrat named Algernon in a painter's studio, where Willie has decided to try his luck as a painter's model.

Of Algernon's first entrance, one detail stands out, "The sun was shining through his fine blond hair."[100] The pair fall in love. Algernon has the idea of laying a tribute of flowers—roses and poppies, of course, among others—at the feet of a statue of Hadrian's beloved Antinous. He prays, "O Antinous, . . . beautiful boy beloved of an emperor, to thee we dedicate our new-found love."[101] Soon, inspired by their love affair, the painter has the idea of painting Parsifal and Galahad praying before the hermit. Willie is to be Parsifal, that most green of the Arthurian knights, and Algernon, of course, Galahad. "This caught the imagination of them all. Algy was just right for Galahad, they said, so pure and golden."[102]

But the romance is short-lived. Algernon's chivalry and high-flown sentiments get stuck on Willie's lower-class origins. He flees commitment and seeks refuge in the golden drill of upper-class engagements from which safe distance he can shower unfortunates like Willie with his philanthropy. Willie is crushed by Algernon's desertion and he returns to his former trade with a vengeance, but his instincts—and a genuine capacity to love and to serve—rescue him in the end and the flower-boy graduates to fully fledged green man.

The portrait of the golden boy Hunt gives us is very precisely observed for all its preposterous aspects. Indeed "preposterous" belongs to the golden boy's lexicon; it is a synonym for "unreal." It is reality or "paying my dues via the dirt," as one golden-boy analysand put it, that he cannot cope with. Beside Algernon could be placed many more fictional examples, equally charming, unreliable, "good"—like the high-minded young Quaker pacifist, Andrew, with hair the color of old gilt, who flees the reality of his deep affection for another man in Mary Renault's *The Charioteer* (1953)—but I think Hunt has given us a clear enough idea of the type.

---

[100] *Street Lavendar,* p. 265.
[101] Ibid., p. 271.
[102] Ibid., p 273.

Roland Against the Piano's Tail, 1952
(from Peter Samuelson, *Post-War Friends*)

The Hellenist

In fact, all the yellow types have an unreality about them, they all evince something of the puer. They don't really like belonging to the world, at least to the present one. This is true even of the summer-sunlight type, whom I call the Hellenist, the most conventional and familiar of the yellow types. This is the yellow man of whom Wilson and Bek speak when they write, "A yellow person probably goes to university and enjoys a life of study."[103] "Probably" is an important qualification, as many such men are students of life—at least from a respectable distance—rather than of literature or science. They are philosophers, seekers after the truth. Giving a certain glow to their search for meaning is the paganism of Hellenic culture, the culture of Plato and Socrates. This paganism was one of "intellectual light," as Walter Pater put it.[104]

Sometimes this influence expresses itself subtly, tacitly, but its presence is nonetheless palpable. A man so influenced shows himself keen on constructing systems and typologies, of trying to grasp the ungraspable. Yet he remains circumspect, graceful, diplomatic; he can appreciate different points of view and himself hold traditional and iconoclastic ideas at the same time with no apparent conflict. Men who pronounce themselves sympathetic to same-sex attachments while maintaining an otherwise conventional emotional and domestic life frequently belong to this type—homoeroticism has a philosophical place in their world. This world is a bit too tidy though, a bit too sure of itself and its inhabitants are difficult to read emotionally—*everything* has its neat little place.

In Forster's novel, Clive Durham, the fair-faced Cambridge scholar who helps Maurice give a name to his troublesome longings, is such a type. Devoutly religious as a boy, he is profoundly shocked by the discovery of his homosexual desires. His response has two typical parts: 1) "It should not ever become carnal," and 2) "Why had he out of all Christians been punished with it?"[105]

> The boy had always been a scholar, awake to the printed word, and the horrors the Bible evoked for him were to be laid by Plato. Never could he forget his emotion at first reading the *Phaedrus.* He saw there his malady described exquisitely, calmly, as a passion which we can direct, like any other, towards good or bad. Here was no invitation to licence. He could not believe his good fortune at first—thought there must be some misunderstanding and that he and Plato were thinking of different things. Then he saw that the temperate pagan really did comprehend him, and, slipping past the Bible rather than opposing it, was offering a new guide for life.[106]

---

[103] *What Colour are You?,* p. 24.
[104] *The Renaissance,* p. 122.
[105] *Maurice,* p. 67.
[106] Ibid., pp. 67-68.

Later in the novel, when Clive contemplates breaking with Maurice, he retreats to his philosophical birthplace:

> Clive sat in the theatre of Dionysos. The stage was empty, as it had been for many centuries, the auditorium empty; the sun had set though the Acropolis behind still radiated heat. He saw barren plains running down to the sea, Salamis, Aegina, mountains, all blended in a violet evening. Here dwelt his gods—Pallas Athene in the first place: he might if he chose imagine her shrine untouched, and her statue catching the last of the glow. She understood all men, though motherless and a virgin. He had been coming to thank her for years because she had lifted him out of the mire.[107]

Clive comes to despise Greece and what it meant for him as he comes to find Maurice contemptible. In so doing, he relinquishes the yellow role to Maurice himself. Clive becomes a blue man, obsessed with his social and especially political position.

> To the end of his life Clive was not sure of the exact moment of departure, and with the approach of old age he grew uncertain whether the moment had yet occurred. The Blue Room [of his club] would glimmer, ferns undulate. Out of some eternal Cambridge his friend began beckoning to him, clothed in the sun, and shaking out the scents and sounds of the May Term.[108]

His beginnings, as this passage suggests ("clothed in the sun"), remain pure Hellenist yellow.

Mann gives us another portrait of the Hellenic man in the writer Gustave Aschenbach, hero of *Death in Venice*.

> Remote on the one hand from the banal, on the other from the eccentric, his genius was calculated to win at once the adhesion of the general public and the admiration, both sympathetic and stimulating, of the connoisseur. From childhood up he was pushed on every side to achievement, and achievement of no ordinary kind, and so his young days never knew the sweet idleness and blithe *laissez aller* that belong to youth.[109]

Discipline mixed with precocity is a quality that also belongs to Clive and many other fictional yellow men. Childhood precocity with Clive takes the form of an endless round of silent questioning—Who am I? What is my task? What is this I'm feeling? How do I integrate these feelings into my life? For Aschenbach, it is a premature recognition of his duty, his destiny. However, where Aschenbach reveals his Hellenic sympathies most emphatically is in his observations on Tadzio whose head recalls to him "the noblest moment of Greek

---

[107] Ibid., p. 104.
[108] Ibid., p. 215.
[109] *Death in Venice and Seven Other Stories*, p. 9.

sculpture," "the head of Eros, with the yellowish bloom of Parian marble,"[110] and who at various times is Phaeax, Narcissus and Hyacinthus.

> When the sun was going down behind Venice, he would sometimes sit on a bench in the park and watch Tadzio, white-clad, with gay-coloured sash, at play there on the rolled gravel with his ball; and at such times it was not Tadzio whom he saw, but Hyacinthus, doomed to die because two gods were rivals for his love. Ah, yes, he tasted the envious pangs that Zephyr knew when his rival, bow and cithara, oracle and all forgot, played with the beauteous youth.[111]

Classical references delineate Aschenbach's world—there is that extraordinary description of dawn where Eos, Orion, Cleithos, Cephalus, Poseidon and Pan all make an appearance—but the most significant is undoubtedly the one to the Socratic dialogue *Phaedrus* which undertakes to establish the relationship of love to beauty in both its earthly and philosophical forms. As we saw, Clive was similarly influenced in his self-discovery. So, too, was Graham Iddlesleigh, the schoolboy hero of a novel by Forrest Reid. In the first flush of his tender friendship with the Dionysian Harold Brocklehurst, he turns to the *Phaedrus,*

> which he had worked through with his father. . . . They had studied together most of the shorter dialogues, and the whole of the *Republic,* but the *Phaedrus* Graham cared for most . . . it *was* poetry! deep, impassioned poetry! . . . Surely no other books were so fair and sweet, so wise and true. In the charmed circle of their range, the coarser quality of things were forgotten, the light was cleansed, the whole realm of the soul lay clear. He knew no other writings that flowed in with so gracious a charm upon one's spirit, filling it with a love for all that is beautiful and good, watering its "wing-feathers": no others that exercised so humanising an influence upon one's character.[112]

For Iddlesleigh as for Clive and Aschenbach, ascent to "those pure, colourless regions, to that radiant world of ideas, by Phaedo's golden hair,"[113] remains the strongest message of the Platonic canon.

For Mary Renault's heroes in the *The Charioteer,* the message is contained rather in the image of the chariot pulled by two horses, one black and unruly, the other noble and white, symbolizing the conflict between bodily and spiritual desires. Early on in the story, yellow Ralph Lanyon as a young man leaves school in disgrace after a love affair with a younger boy. Laurie, his green counterpart at school, defends him and earns for his efforts a copy of the *Phaedrus.* Years later,

---

[110] Ibid., p. 29.
[111] Ibid., pp. 49-50.
[112] *The Garden God: A Tale of Two Boys,* pp. 59-61.
[113] Ibid., p. 61.

in a hospital following the allied defeat at Dunkirk, Laurie rediscovers Ralph's gift at just the point when Andrew, the Quaker orderly, enters his life to claim his love.[114] The *Phaedrus* becomes a kind of leitmotif in the novel and indeed provides Renault with her fadeout image over Ralph and Laurie's dramatic reunion:

> Quietly as night shuts down the uncertain prospect of the road ahead, the wheels sink to stillness in the dust of the halting place, and the reins drop from the driver's loosened hands. Staying each his hunger on what pasture the place affords them, neither the white horse nor the black reproaches his fellow for drawing their master out of the way. They are far, both of them, from home, and lonely, and lengthened by their strife the way has been hard. Now their heads droop side by side till their long manes mingle; and when the voice of the charioteer falls silent they are reconciled for a night in sleep.[115]

When a man gives a gift of the *Phaedrus,* it is not surprising to find him described as Renault describes the young Ralph: "He was slight and lean, with dusty-fair hair and eyes of a striking light blue which were narrowed by the structure of the orbit above, giving him a searching look even when he smiled";[116] or,

> The biggest toughs in the School, when they stood against Lanyon, looked muscle-bound or run to seed. Lines of decision showed around his eyes and mouth; at nineteen, he was marked already with the bleak courage of the self-disciplined neurotic. Laurie, who was in no state to be analytical, only thought that Lanyon looked more than usually liked chilled steel.[117]

Ralph could easily be one of Aschenbach's heroes who demonstrate "an intellectual and virginal manliness, which clenches its teeth and stands in modest defiance of the swords and spears that pierce its side."[118] In Ralph's dignified presence, Laurie is lifted

> into a kind of exalted dream, part loyalty, part hero-worship, all romance. Half remembered images moved in it, the tents of Troy, the columns of Athens, David waiting in an olive grove for the sound of Jonathan's bow.[119]

It is perhaps worth noting here that the similarity—striking, to say the least—among the heroes created by Forster, Mann, Reid and Renault (like that

---

[114] *The Charioteer,* pp. 112ff.

[115] Ibid., pp. 393-394.

[116] Ibid., p. 29.

[117] Ibid.

[118] *Death in Venice and Seven Other Stories,* p. 11.

[119] Renault, *The Charioteer,* p. 36.

among the flower boys we spoke of earlier) is owing entirely to their archetypal source. Our Hellenist type of homosexual man is descended from the sort of hero we find in fairy tales as prince or king-to-be, struggling against almost insurmountable odds to gain the treasure that is his. He is a relative of the sun gods of ancient mythology who experienced death and renewal as an inevitable—even daily—life pattern.

This type must grasp what is happening to him in words, concepts, images; he needs a philosophical position. The golden boy can simply assail the windmills of life, armed only with a passionate idealism; the Hellenic man needs a stouter weapon. Reason as a moral virtue, reason as it was celebrated in the so-called Age of Enlightenment and, indeed, in all classical and neoclassical epochs; reason as light and illumination is that weapon. Not, I wish to emphasize, the empiricism and logic of the man-of-sciences, the blue man, but Reason.

The Lunatic

De Vries has differentiated two types of light: sun, symbolizing nature manifest, and moon, symbolizing the occult side of nature.[120] It is the whitish-yellow light of the moon, a "reflected" light, that best fits our third type of yellow man, the Lunatic type. He is not necessarily lunatic in the sense of bedlam—though he may well be—but he does move on the fringes of the daylight world, an interloper, profoundly ill-at-ease with hard forms, with precise and reasonable phenomena. It's not that he despises reason or philosophy, it's just that his philosophy seeks, like moonlight, to blend forms together rather than separate them, to find the correspondences within the world of forms. To do this, he uses mostly words and images—like the Hellenist—but as the artist, poet, mystic and healer uses them, exploring the unconscious sources, their origins.

As an artist, he differs from the red man, the man-of-arts, in his emphasis on process rather than product, on the journey rather than the arrival. The lunatic artist sees a painting or poem as only a step, a tentative step towards realizing the mysterious, inner kingdom. The symbolist-aesthetic movement of the *fin-de-siècle* which Mackintosh has called, "a deliberate assault on conventional life in the name of hidden truth,"[121] illustrates the lunatic artist's way.

Only a lunatic artist could write,

> There by a dim and dark Lethaen well
>   Young Charmides was lying, wearily
> He plucked the blossoms from the asphodel,
> And with its little rifled treasury
> Strewed the dull waters of the dusky stream,

120 *Dictionary of Symbols and Imagery.*
121 *Symbolism and Art Nouveau,* p. 39.

And watched the white stars founder, and the land was like a dream.[122]

The Hellenic type, though often a writer, is never seduced to such extremes. His poetry radiates rather the light of a sunlit world—or utter darkness; there is no twilight for him.

As a mystic, the lunatic type has visions on the order of St. John's:

> At once I was in the Spirit, and lo, a throne stood in heaven, with one seated on the throne! And he who sat there appeared like jasper and carnelian, and round the throne was a rainbow that looked like emerald.[123]

Or he has miraculous experiences like St. Philip Neri's swallowing of a flaming sphere. Both express a similar super-heightened symbolic grasp of life's meaning. John, it must be remembered, was the evangelist for whom light became synonymous with the Word of God and the Son of Man; both his gospel and the Apocalypse play mystical variations on this theme. Philip Neri's experience made a similar link between word and light and today he is remembered as the founder of an order of priests noted for their oratory in the pulpit, the Oratorians. The man most responsible for the spread of the Oratorian Movement in Britain was, of course, the eloquent John Henry, later Cardinal, Newman. He, too, showed an understanding of light as a mystical experience of the Word, as this lovely prayer I recall from childhood suggests: "Stay with me, O Lord, and then I will begin to shine, as Thou shinest, so to shine, as to be a light unto others."

As both artist and mystic, the lunatic type speaks of the inner light, an unpredictable, often diffuse flame that can nonetheless burn with almost unbearable intensity. It is this light that seems to torment Francis Croft, the mad poet of *The Bird of Night* (1972).

Behind all such figures we can detect the voice of Orpheus singing. Orpheus, as Ovid depicts him, post-Eurydice, playing his lyre on a shadeless tract of ground; "But when the bard, / The heaven-born bard, sat there and touched his strings, / Shade came in plenty. Every tree was there."[124] This same Orpheus appears numerous times as a subject for symbolist painters and poets. The Belgian symbolist Jean Delville painted him, following his dismemberment by the Maenads, as a head floating down to Lesbos on the lyre, still singing. This head, haloed by a mass of silken curls, glows an iridescent whitish yellow and resembles nothing so much as a constellation fallen from the night sky. Placed in a shrine at Lesbos, it becomes the focus of an Orphic cult, which will contribute an opalescent thread to the tapestry of late-Western occultism. Mixed up

---

[122] Oscar Wilde, "Charmides," *Complete Works of Oscar Wilde,* p. 769.

[123] Rev. 4: 2-3.

[124] *Metamorphoses,* book 10, p. 227.

with the mystery cult, we encounter—not surprisingly—considerable homoeroticism. As Ovid explains,

> Three times the sun had reached the watery Fish
> That close the year, while Orpheus held himself
> Aloof from love of women, hurt perhaps
> By ill-success or bound by plighted troth.
> Yet many a woman burned with passion for
> The bard, and many grieved at their repulse.
> It was his lead that taught the folk of Thrace
> The love for tender boys, to pluck the buds,
> The brief springtime, with manhood still to come.[125]

What concerns us here, besides the relationship of Orpheus to homosexual passion, is the disembodied nature of the prophet's song. Our lunatic type, like the golden boy, is not comfortable on the ground; like the music or the poem he makes, he must soar. He is often mistaken—incorrectly—for a puer. The puer may play a part in his creativity, but the lunatic's chief influences are much darker than the puer can admit to consciously. The American artist Paul Cadmus, in a painting entitled *Le Ruban Dénoué*, a homage to turn-of-the-century French salon composer Reynaldo Hahn, pinpoints the exact nature of the lunatic's influences. Hahn, mid-composition, is shown receiving a kiss from his "angelic essence," while at his feet sprawls a leering and irrepressibly aroused Pan. (Hahn, incidentally, was noted mainly for his vocal music.)

The lunatic type is actually much closer to the flower boy, at least in terms of his fragility, his morbid sensitivity. Not infrequently, he also loves such a boy for his darkly delicate beauty. He himself is not beautiful, though occasionally he will be associated to a flower, usually a white flower:

> For you a House of Ivory,
>   (Roses are white in the rose-bower)!
> A narrow bed for me to lie,
>   (White, O white, is the hemlock flower)![126]

But it is with birds that the lunatic type is most often associated, as we find in Wilde's "Vita Nuova":

> I stood by the unvintageable sea
>   Till the wet waves drenched face and hair with spray;
> The long red fires of the dying day
> Burned in the west; the wind piped drearily;
> And to the land the clamorous gulls did flee:
>   "Alas!" I cried, "my life is full of pain . . ."[127]

---

125 Ibid.
126 Wilde, "Chanson," *Complete Works of Oscar Wilde*, p. 752.
127 Ibid., p. 811.

Oscar Wilde (1854-1900), 1882
(The Bettmann Archive; photograph by Sarony)

Or as in Susan Hill's *The Bird of Night,* where Francis is seen "striding like a crane over the beach" in his carpet slippers to buy fish.[128] Francis is haunted by dreams of rapacious birds and the memory of an owl flying through the dead of a winter's night. Later, Francis and his lover Harvey install themselves in a London flat where, like a cliff-dwelling bird, Francis constructs himself a nest at the top of the house, "looking down on to the garden . . . between high piles of books."[129] Harvey even terms it an eyrie. The bird imagery emphasizes the lunatic's feeling of discomfort with his own body, a discomfort bordering on the grotesque and macabre. Francis himself refers to his own body as

a polyp. . . . I feel every day as if I shall burst open and spew out anyhow from the bag of my skin and leave only bone. I am all bones and bones break. I think of myself lying in my tomb, a pile of bones.[130]

Sometimes the lunatic type is even handicapped in some way, usually lame, a kind of wounded healer whose Orphic song cures all. The bird imagery also points to the spiritual qualities of this type, to their special abilities:

Imagination, memory, the musical gift, that is all. And the eye which links not A to B but A to P or Z, which is rarer.[131]

The lunatic type's nearest relative in the world of fairy tales is probably the nightingale. From Old Persia, we have a tale (which inspired another from Oscar Wilde) about a nightingale pierced in the heart by a thorn of the white rose it loves. It bleeds to death, singing of its passion, and as it does it stains the white rose red. Thus, Persian story-tellers accounted for the relationship of the red rose to Eros and passion. In Hans Christian Andersen's beautiful story "The Nightingale," the glorious song of a simple, brown nightingale rescues his former master from the brink of death. This master, no less than the Emperor of China, had earlier replaced it for a sparkling, bejewelled imitation that showed its true mettle by breaking down at the very moment the Emperor needed it. In similar ways is the lunatic type by his unprepossessing, even absurd, appearance, mocked, neglected, misunderstood, and his role as outsider and interloper reinforced.

I have mentioned already the importance of moonlight in understanding the yellow of this particular type, particularly the diffuse, occult aspects. I should only like to add that moonlit nights in the world of yellow-green relations are as inspiring to love and confessions of love as in heterosexual romances. One might say that on moonlit nights, we all tend to behave like lunatics. (Is this

---

128 *The Bird of Night,* p. 46.
129 Ibid., p. 123.
130 Ibid., p. 32.
131 Ibid., p. 93.

just another way of saying that all lovers are poets?) Harvey's night of greatest happiness with Francis was moonlit:

> It was a very calm sea and then the moon came riding gracefully out from behind the clouds and sent a shiver of light across the glistening surface. I saw Francis's tall figure standing right down at the edge of the water. I heard him laughing to himself.[132]

In Xavier Mayne's *Imre* (1906), several major communications between the two would-be lovers, the eponymous hero, a Hungarian soldier, and an American man-of-the-world, take place under the influence of a night sky. The latter's long account of his Uranistic development, for example, is accompanied by "the sweep of the night-wind . . . among the acacias" and the flitting of "the birds of shadow."[133] In the final scene, following Imre's own confession of homosexuality—this was an era when such confessions were still earth-shattering—the two prepare to rest, united at last; the American Oswald remembers it thus:

> We were back in the quiet room, lighted now only by the moon. Far up, on the distant Pálota heights, the clear bell of Szent-Mátyás struck the three-quarters. The slow notes filled the still night like a benediction, keyed to that haunting, divine, prophetic triad, Life—Love—Death! Benediction threefold and supreme to the world![134]

This is pure lunatic exaltation. And, finally, in Forster's novel, Maurice is propelled by a disturbing dream into a lunatic invocation of love—

> He moaned, half asleep. There was something better in life than this rubbish, if only he could get to it—love—nobility—big spaces where passion clasped peace, spaces no science could reach, but they existed for ever, full of woods some of them, and arched with majestic sky and a friend. . . .
>
> He really was asleep when he sprang up and flung wide the curtains with a cry of "Come!" The action awoke him; what had he done that for? A mist covered the grass of the park, and the tree trunks rose out of it like the channel marks in the estuary near his old private school. It was jolly cold. He shivered and clenched his fists. The moon had risen.[135]

His summons is answered a few minutes later by the appearance of the game-keeper Scudder at his window. Voice thick with fear and desire, Scudder whispers, "Sir, was you calling out for me? . . . Sir, I know . . . I know,"[136] and then he touches Maurice. Between the moonlit world where shines the lunatic and lunatic inspiration, seeking a vessel, a recipient, an acknowledgment, and the

---

[132] Ibid., p. 45.
[133] *Imre: A Memorandum,* p. 151.
[134] Ibid., p. 204.
[135] *Maurice,* p. 167.
[136] Ibid.

earthy world of the green gardener waiting for a spark, a jolt, a warmth, there exists a special sympathy which we shall investigate a little further on.

Apollo, Yellow's God

The god ruling all three types of yellow man is obviously Apollo. He is the *kouros* par excellence, the beautiful ephebe and golden boy to whom we owe the popular expression, "He's a real Apollo." He is also sun-god, aloof, radiating power; as well as the father of Orpheus, god of music and of prophecy and supervisor of the Muses ("Apollon musagète," as Stravinsky and Balanchine called him). And, he is also the lover of young men, two at least, Hyacinthus and Cyparissus. He is well qualified to be the lover of youths as he himself served for a time as shepherd to King Admetus whose eromenos (beloved) he became.

With Apollo, we are much closer to father's than to mother's realm, father, of course, being Zeus. Apollo's sojourn in Admetus's court was in fact a punishment imposed by father Zeus after his ill-tempered slaying of the Cyclopes. It seems to be generally the case with yellow men that father and his realm play a more formative role than does mother, even, or perhaps especially, when father is negative, as he is, for instance, in *The Bird of Night* for Francis. Mother is often ineffectual, but she can also be, at the same time even, evil in her lack of appropriate mothering behavior. She is a hollow, theatrical mother who substitutes the dramatic gesture for real feeling. This kind of mother loves seemingly unmoved by the mother archetype, a twisted, semi-mad product of the patriarchy.

Apollo's mother, the Titaness Leto, conforms to this picture insofar as her life is not her own; it is at the mercy of Zeus' pleasure (and Hera's jealousy). She must fight for every inch of ground she gains and sometimes her tactics, the birth of Apollo and Artemis for example, are, to put it mildly, dramatic.

The modern Irish writer Jennifer Johnston paints an extremely harsh portrait of the yellow mother in *How Many Miles to Babylon?* This is a woman, her son Alexander tells us, who

> had a contrived radiance which strangers took for reality, but which to me seemed to be a thin shell covering some black burning rage which constantly consumed her. When she played the piano, she played with an anger that made me uneasy, made me have to leave the room out of some kind of fear, listen from a safe distance.[137]

After shaming her yellow son (lunatic type) into enlisting in the First World War, she treats him to a shameless farewell.

> Mother was standing in the drawing-room waiting for me. She threw out her arms as I came in with a splendidly theatrical gesture. I walked towards her.

---

[137] *How Many Miles to Babylon?*, p. 35.

The room seemed about a mile long. I finally reached her and her hands flew like two birds around my neck and she pulled my face down to hers. I kissed one cheek and then the other. She still held me. I put up my hands and unfastened hers. Her eyes were the most triumphant blue.[138]

Angered by "the mutual pleasure given and received between my father and myself,"[139] this mother plants a poisonous seed in her son's mind on the eve of his departure for the war, consisting of the notion that the man he believes to be his father is perhaps not his father at all. Alexander tries to reject the notion, but she only laughs a little and says, "Run along, dear boy, you'll miss your train."[140] His father, by contrast, presents a far more sympathetic face, one turned to the Irish earth and the people who till it. He admonishes Alexander,

I would like to know that you will always do what is best for the land. Not for you or her or the strange dreams that may come into your head. Here, the land must come first. You understand. It is this country's heart. It was taken from the people. We . . . I must be clear . . . We took it from the people. I would like to feel that it will, when the moment comes, be handed back in good order.[141]

When John Hilliard, the yellow man hero of Susan Hill's *Strange Meeting* (1971), takes leave of his parents to return to the trenches in France, he remarks how his father "was becoming obsessive about the state of the lawns," baked yellow after weeks of hot summer, and paced "about them each morning and evening, poking with his stick, and holding bitter, repetitive conversations with Plummet."[142] His mother meanwhile looks on, dressed as if she were going to "some wedding—or garden party or dinner or opera . . . a provincial woman who bought the type of clothes designed for some London society hostess."

Once, his mother's hair had been butter-coloured, but he could scarcely remember that, she had gone grey very early. Now the sun made it glint with a curiously artificial light, like something concocted out of wire and floss by a theatrical wig-maker. She was a tall woman, tightly corseted, upright. But not graceful, though she always wore graceful clothes, which flowed and folded about her, she was fondest of silks and cashmere and lawn. Her dress today was of lawn, pale cream, with full sleeves and a high neck, bands of lace. . . . As a boy he had been embarrassed by the grandeur of her costume, when she came to see him at school.[143]

---

138 Ibid., p. 69.
139 Ibid., p. 35.
140 Ibid., p. 69.
141 Ibid., pp. 42-43.
142 *Strange Meeting*, p. 27.
143 Ibid.

Jean Broc, *The Death of Hyacinth*
(Musée des Beaux-Arts, Poitiers)

Similarly, in *Maurice,* the two widowed mothers—Clive's and Maurice's—are mannequins, old dolls speaking the notions expected of them by the patriarchy. Clive's mother, in particular, is dry, a "Clive with the sap perished."[144] Just prior to his night of passion with Clive's gamekeeper, Maurice watches Mrs. Durham through the window, "all relaxed and ugly. Her face clicked into position as he entered, so did his own."[145]

In contrast, the green man's mother is never so sharply defined; her presence is felt rather as a diffuse source of comfort and support. It is through his mother's legacy—she died on Armistice Day—that Harvey is able to provide a home for Francis in *The Bird of Night.* In *How Many Miles to Babylon?* and *Strange Meeting,* the green man's mother appears only as the author of letters, but these are letters full of love, so that we cannot speak of absence when we refer to her as we most certainly can of the more present mother of the yellow man. Take the example of Miriam Barton's letter to John Hilliard, a man she does not know except through her own son's missives from the trenches:

> We are so much longing to see you. What will the arrangements be? We hope you will be able to stay here for a few days or even longer. Come now, you *will,* won't you? We know you cannot have anything more pressing. You are not to think of the future at all just now, you are still convalescing and everyone is going to make sure that you are looked after and not troubled at all by anything. . . . Oh, you cannot think how much we look forward to seeing you, how much this will mean to us! Or perhaps you can? Yes, I think so.[146]

Miriam Barton knows Hilliard loved her son; for her, that is all that finally matters. In grateful return, she connects him to the positive mother he missed.

Although his relationship to mother is problematic, leaving him prey at times to severe father complexes, the yellow man finds some solace in a strong and usually positive relationship with his sister. Apollo again provides the model through his twinship with Artemis, who is, not so incidentally, a moon goddess. The yellow man and his sister appear as an important constellation in numerous mythological and literary accounts of the green-yellow attraction. Among them are the Biblical Jonathan and his sister Michal (who becomes David's wife), Orestes and Electra (who becomes Pylades' wife), Frantz de Galais and Yvonne in Alain-Fournier's *Le grand Meaulnes,* Jan and Vivian in Mary Renault's *Purposes of Love* (1939), and Hilliard and Beth in *Strange Meeting.*

Occasionally it is the green man's sister, as with the young "cabbage-head" Raleigh in Sherriff's war drama, *Journey's End* (1928), or, in Maurice's green

---

[144] *Maurice,* p. 162.
[145] Ibid., p. 166.
[146] *Strange Meeting,* p. 177.

phase, his sister Ada, who tempts the yellow man, but this relationship is seldom consummated. Rather she serves in the same fashion as the yellow man's sister, as a symbol of the affectional bond between the green and the yellow men. She testifies to the blood-brother intensity of their relationship. We see this vividly played out in Yves Navarre's *Le petit galopin de nos corps* (The Urchin of our Bodies; 1977), where the heroes, Roland (yellow) and Joseph (green), in an effort to find a container for their fierce passion, a constraint rather, marry sisters and so become brothers. The sister testifies to the intensity of the relationship and, at the same time, can signal a retreat from that intensity. This is true not only of Sabine and Clothilde in the Navarre novel, but also of Ada Hall who is the first target of Clive's shift in affections from Maurice. Very often, too, such sisters have a Muse-like function, inspiring a creative resolution of the green-yellow bond.

If we look at Artemis as an aspect of Apollo, we can, I think, get a clearer picture of the yellow man's attitude to his fleshly side. The myth of Actaeon shows us an Artemis horrified, enraged at being seen naked while bathing by the handsome young hunter. In her fury, she turns him into a stag and he is torn apart by his own hounds. Her horror we might understand as a fear of being seen in her weakness, that is, her human form. The green man who has no fear or shame regarding such weakness in himself—in fact, it is rather a source of strength and trust or faith than otherwise—often assumes the same trust exists in the yellow. The yellow man, however, has little confidence in the mother world, scant comprehension of a "body-self," as Neumann calls it, and such an assumption on the part of the green can provoke him to ferocious, cruel, sometimes life-destroying retaliation. I think Hill suggests something of this sort in *Strange Meeting*. Hilliard has just met his new second-in-command, David Barton, a young man whose openness and love of life puzzles Hilliard, fascinates him and, at the same time, makes him wary, frightened, angry.

"I imagine it was fairly painful?"

Hilliard glanced up, startled. Barton was looking with interest at the red, rough-edged scar along his left thigh. It made him want to conceal it hurriedly, he felt ashamed in some odd way, it seemed a blemish, a flaw, for which he was accountable. The only people to look at it until now had been the doctors, and that was not the same thing. He himself had examined it, peering at it closely as he used to peer at scabs and bruises on arms and knees when he was a small boy, charting their progress from blue to brown to yellow, watching the thickening of the skin. He touched this shrapnel wound with the pads of his fingers, sitting on his bed at Hawton, and now Barton was looking at it with the same kind of curiosity.

"You'll see a lot worse than this," Hilliard said shortly, reaching for his pyjamas.

"But that's not the point, is it? I've never seen any shrapnel wound before, this is the first."

"You must have seen plenty of gore in your father's surgery."
"That was different. Isn't this different, for you? It's your own injury,
that's the one you know about, that's the one that counts. Only by that can
you assess what other people suffer, surely. By the damage to your own
flesh, by the amount of pain *you* feel."[147]

Hilliard is amazed at Barton's perspicacity—"Hilliard thought, how does he
know?"[148] He has never met its like before. *Strange Meeting* traces Hilliard's
growing openness to Barton (culminating in love) and its concomitant acceptance of the underlying challenge of the green man, to love one's humanness
fully. But, this is taking us too far ahead.

The vengeful Artemis face of the Apollonian yellow man, as it appears in the
realm of his body attitudes, brings up the issue of the shadow. This shadow is
not, as so many seem to think, Dionysus (or Pan or Priapus) just as the Apollonian is not the shadow of the green man's Dionysian side. They are two halves
of a whole, in the Platonic sense; to call them shadow is to minimize their importance for each other. Yes, Apollo is responsible for killing the satyr Marsyas,
and for coaxing, or, better, conning the art of prophecy out of Pan, but these acts
do not make his victim into a shadow. His sometimes violent and calculating,
one might say cold-blooded, ways of behaving—these belong to his shadow. It
is a violence that expresses itself as either a burning or a scorching—too much
light, too much heat—or as a Plutonic eclipse of light where the victim is sen-
tenced to isolation in a cold and loveless space. Such is Clive's treatment of
Maurice when he falls out of love with him and goes seeking a wife:

> His ideal of marriage was temperate and graceful, like all his ideals, and he
> found a fit helpmate in Anne, who had refinement herself, and admired it in
> others. They loved each other tenderly. Beautiful conventions received
> them—while beyond the barrier Maurice wandered, the wrong words on his
> lips and the wrong desires in his heart, and his arms full of air.[149]

Eugene Monick links Apollo with what he calls solar phallos. Its shadow,
which he, too, distinguishes from the Dionysian, can lead, he writes,

> to a degree of destruction only hinted at by shadow chthonic phallos be-
> haviour. The highest potential of masculine solar consciousness—spiritual-
> ity, intellectual and institutional leadership—can tyrannize whatever is con-
> sidered to be in error, whoever cannot "measure up" (an oblique reference to
> the interest males have in phallic size). The tyranny is all the more devas-
> tating due to the cultural admiration of solar masculine attributes, behind
> which the shadow qualities fester.[150]

---

147 Ibid., pp. 58-59.
148 Ibid., p. 59.
149 *Maurice,* p. 144.
150 *Phallos,* p. 106.

We will see later how the so-called Great War provided a vivid illustration of the collective solar phallic shadow. Monick continues,

Ideological principles are indigenous to solar masculinity. They have the ring of truth about them, but the underside, the shadow, of righteousness and purity is organized mayhem and death.[151]

The only problem with this account of Apollonian values—and Monick is not the only writer to see them as a reflection of the "straight and narrow"[152] or of "straight-arrow, regularly defined, progressively linear"[153] phallos—is that it leaves out much that belongs to Apollo's divinity. Music, the arts, prophecy and healing are anything but "straight-arrow" or "regularly defined" activities. What Monick is describing here is closer to my concept of the blue man. Nevertheless, his point is well put. Like the green man who becomes something of a conservative and dogmatist when he mixes too much with blue, rational values, so too the yellow man, very easily contaminated, as Goethe said, can turn into a brutal authoritarian, especially when he surrenders his own insights or standpoint to be used by an uncomprehending blue cultural position. When I spoke of the green man as dictator, I had in mind Fascist or Communist party functionaries (the sort of men recently exposed in Romania and other Eastern bloc countries). The yellow man's dictator shadow has a more sovereign quality, high-handed, contemptuous; he destroys life easily, without flinching and without feeling the need to justify himself with textbook ideology.

To summarize the many hues of the yellow type, we might quote a description of him in Vannier where he is called, naturally enough, "the Apollonian":

Sober, little inclined to sensuality, fleeing excess and only giving what is absolutely necessary to physical needs, the Apollonian nonetheless spends a lot of energy on his "toilette." As much as his private life is simple, he loves to surround himself with luxury and opulence when he is obliged to make public appearances. He is born to be rich. Poverty is unendurable; his nature is too precious, too highly evolved to support well the material struggles of life.[154]

Wilson and Bek corroborate the yellow man's disdain of physical necessities when they write, "Yellow people tend to ignore the body. They enjoy food but possibly not if they have to cook it constantly."[155] Vannier continues, "The Apollonian loves to shine forth and to protect. He needs light. The sun is for

151 Ibid.
152 Ibid., p. 88.
153 Ibid., p. 89.
154 *La typologie,* p. 103.
155 *What Colour are You?,* p. 24.

him a powerful revitalizing force."[156] His love of light can be seen in his activities, which Scott lists as "projective . . . expansive, aspiring, investigatory," and their affective aspects, "variability, expectancy, originality, exhilaration."[157] The revitalizing potency of light for the yellow man brings relaxation, a release from "burdens, problems, harassment or restriction"[158] imposed by the world of matter.

To this picture we might add the light-seeking qualities of the zodiac's fire signs, especially that of the centaur Sagittarius, whose ninth-house residency indicates religious quests, higher consciousness and higher education—not to mention long journeys, for the yellow man is a wanderer, if not physically then mentally and spiritually. Mindell reminds us that the yellow chakra, Manipura, which rules the solar plexus and is known as the lustrous gem, takes for its symbol the ram of Agni, Indian god of fire.[159] This, of course, links it to the Greco-Roman god Mars, governor of the first fire sign in the Western zodiac, Aries. With both Agni and Aries, impulsiveness and violence are dominant; they thus represent a more archaic manifestation of our yellow man's heat and light. But, whatever their degree or kind, heat and light are the ruling principles of the yellow man's world. At the same time, as we've seen, he can be remarkably cool, aloof, effectively absent.

I spoke of the green man as being sometimes dreamy. This quality can give him a kind of distance, as though his ear were turned Amerindian style to the earth, listening to its deep, distant murmurings, rumblings, groans and sighs and translating them into handwork. But, he rarely communicates—unless hurt—aloofness. Aloofness pertains to the heights where the yellow resides, one might say perches. We all know quick-minded, penetrating, intellectual, imaginative, intuitive men who float in a baroque world of blue skies peopled with shining creatures and are simply not present. We may blame their aloofness on idealism, perfectionism, a luxuriant creative imagination, but we cannot explain it away or coax them easily to ground. Even in sex, such men tend to live in the head, in the image—a Proustian remembrance of the event, rather than the event itself. Vannier puts it admirably:

> He loves lyrically. He finds in love inspiration for his art. He also loves perversely, i.e., suffering and making the Other suffer often for the mere thrill of it; he seeks incessantly after new voluptuous sensations. The urgency of his desire to please often stops with possession.[160]

---

[156] *La typologie,* p. 104.
[157] *The Lüscher Color Test,* p. 34.
[158] Ibid.
[159] *Dreambody,* p. 41.
[160] *La typologie,* p. 24.

Was it in the name of such a possession that Hyacinthus was sacrificed? But Vannier closes his description of the Apollonian man, so similar in many ways to Jung's description of the intuitive type, on quite another note: "But he may also sacrifice himself to a high ideal. He is the inspired one who both rouses and sustains through the radiant force of his vision."[161]

We will close here with the yellow man, too.

Conclusion

Of course, what I have been trying to image in the foregoing portraits of green and yellow types does not exist in life in such a pure way. With green, as with yellow men, the different faces of the type blend together, so that we can encounter flower-boy, gardener and prophet-of-the-land aspects mixed in the same man. To these an admixture from the red-blue axis can produce a hybrid. A green man mixed with red, for example, might reveal a passionate humanitarianism or socially and politically conscious attitudes within the framework of architecture or town planning or some kind of artisanship.

One of the leading figures of the Arts and Crafts Movement in *fin-de-siècle* England, William Morris, I could imagine as such a type. Already in 1879, he had said, "Real art is the expression by man of his pleasure in labour."[162] Morris, Service recounts, "wanted a return to idealized medieval days when artists were ordinary working men whose 'daily labour was sweetened by the daily creation of Art.' "[163] One need only turn to Morris's beautiful textiles, furnishings, publications, all of them demonstrating a deep reverence for and love of nature, to see confirmed the possibility of combining socialist humanitarian philosophy with workmanship, not to say artistry, of the highest order.

Red and green might blend in a religious crusade as well, one conducted with a full respect for the instinctive, corporeal man as well as for the devotee; a crusade like that undertaken by Parsifal. According to many accounts, the Grail, containing the scarlet elixir, the blood of Christ, is a chalice of emerald, of green crystal or simply a green stone. (Note, too, that the throne in St. John's vision quoted earlier is both jasper green and carnelian red.) One could continue indefinitely with such proposals—not only with green but also yellow. The only place where our imagination is somewhat limited is in blendings of yellow and green within the same figure. They do occur, but only after considerable struggle; they are opposites, after all.

---

[161] Ibid. Compare Jung: "The intuitive function is represented in consciousness by an attitude of expectancy, by vision and penetration." ("General Description of the Types," *Psychological Types*, CW 6, par. 610)

[162] Alastair Service, *Edwardian Architecture*, p. 12.

[163] Ibid., p. 14.

The plan is clear, I think. I have been describing types, not people. For convenience sake, however, I should like to use these types as a basis for the next step of my investigation, namely, how do green and yellow come together, or, more importantly, for what purpose?

The next chapter will examine in some detail the two principal forms in which we find green-yellow partnerships: the man-boy relationship and that of comrades-in-arms. In the last chapter I present some case material to illustrate the pertinence of this archetypal bond to the psychology of modern men.

The Woodpecker
Tapestry designed by
William Morris
(William Morris Gallery,
Walthamstow, Essex)

Henry Scott Tuke, *Three Companions*, 1905
(from Emmanuel Cooper, *The Life and Work of Henry Scott Tuke*)

3
Green Men with Yellow Men

Two Kinds of Consciousness

Richard Le Gallienne, writing in 1896 of the decade's aesthetic sensibilities, insisted, "Of course, a love for green implies some regard for yellow."[164] Goethe claimed, "The juxtaposition of yellow and green has always something ordinary, but in a cheerful sense."[165] Lüscher color theory puts yellow and green opposite each other, as mutually compensatory in terms of their qualities and effects, while the oriental chakra system places them side by side in the center of the body, solar plexus and heart respectively.

However, their relationship is actually much deeper than any of these juxtapositions implies. In fact, I would suggest that green and yellow, as Earth Mother and Sky Father, are the principal players in many of the world's creation myths; their union or coniunctio is Creation itself. In Old China, to offer but one example, green and yellow were invoked by priests of the sun god as "the animistic world spirit, the forces of nature called . . . the Kwei Shin,"

> the first signifying the contracting principle as exhibited in the Lares Rustici, the nymphs of hills and streams, the grosser spirits of the dead, the second being the expansive force, the spirits of the upper air and the finer part of the spirit in men. These two have to some extent different characteristics, the Kwei for instance responding to ritual while the Shin are properly invoked by music; but in practice they are inseparable, complementary opposites of the same order, and in magical ceremony they are addressed together.[166]

These players were at one time equally valued, each having its own indispensable role, but with the, some would say inevitable, coup by patriarchal powers, the green mother and all her attributes—material, dark, receptive, etc.—came to be devalued. The lower world no longer referred only to a place, both symbolic and real, but carried with it moral disapprobation. The upper world was dominant and indeed its adherents continue, though with increasing difficulty, to insist on its superiority.

I do not intend to argue this world view, which Jung and some of his disciples, notably Erich Neumann, supported and amplified, but only mention it as

---

[164] Jackson, *The Eighteen Nineties,* p. 169.
[165] *Theory of Colours,* p. 324.
[166] John Michell, *The Earth Spirit: Its Ways, Shrines and Mysteries,* p. 20.

the one responsible for the overvaluation of the upper or yellow at the expense of the lower or green, and for the subsequent fascination the green has had for yellow. When speaking of their relationship, I take for granted their equality.

For me, green and yellow represent two kinds of consciousness and unconsciousness, two kinds of spirit and matter, creativity and receptivity, light and darkness. Monet's image (in Eva Figes's novel, *Light*) of an envelope where light is the container and nature the contained—a reversal of the usual roles—is a nice illustration of the possibilities opened for us by a poetic approach to such questions as primordial creativity. Green, in Monet's cosmos, would become the thrusting, aspiring one, restless for the embrace of the yellow or light, desirous of experiencing its own impact. And in the yearning of the green, yellow would see and feel itself given form, given substance.

It is not then just a question of a creative yang, yellow, acting on and penetrating a receptive yin, green, who or which then conceives, gestates and bears yellow's child, but of a mutual fertilization, resulting in a two-parent offspring—a *lumen naturae* perhaps, belonging strictly neither to sky nor to earth, to yellow nor to green.

Some may shake their heads and point to the biological model of mating as to incontrovertible evidence, and I can only say that such a model cannot be used to censor psychic phenomena. Although we see their operation closely in the mating of sky with earth, green and yellow are, for us, primarily psychic energies or values bound in eternal erotic interplay—where one is, so must the other be. They are the crucial coordinates in any genuinely creative endeavor. Whenever one is too highly valued, the other is forced to operate as if it were independent; it is hobbled, it becomes short sighted and the creative act proves impotent. Sometimes the repressed, devalued, dissociated one will retaliate, perhaps leading to a righting of the balance, perhaps causing mayhem and even death (as Aschenbach found out in *Death in Venice*). But whatever happens, the two can never stop relating to each other, even during an enforced separation.

We will be speaking here primarily of green and yellow energies at work between and within men. Thus we are allowed to see them freed to some extent from gender-related evaluations promoted by patriarchal propagandists. At least, we can see green as an energy independent of women who are so often expected to embody it regardless of whether or not it is right for them. However, we must keep in mind that the relationship of yellow to green is everywhere in evidence. Jane Austen, for example, in a letter to her sister, Cassandra, hints that there are green and yellow women. She has been to a showing of portraits in London where she scrutinized the canvases for resemblances to Jane and Elizabeth Bennet, the sister-heroines of her most famous novel, *Pride and Prejudice*. One portrait reminds her of Jane. She writes:

She is dressed in a white gown, with green ornaments, which convinces me of what I had already supposed, that green was a favourite colour with her. I daresay Mrs D. will be in yellow.[167]

This distinction will come as no surprise to those who know the novel, as Jane is the slow, steady, accepting one and Elizabeth ("Mrs D.") the sprightly, temperamental, questioning one.[168]

One might also interpret the energies behind such opposing political and so-cio-economic systems as capitalism (although for Americans money means only green) and socialism as yellow and green. Green was certainly a force to be reckoned with in the late 1960s when capitalism's glinting value system based on the gold standard was challenged by the advent of "flower power"; and it remains a considerable force in such manifestations as the green parties of Europe and other environmental-protection lobbies, where the enemy is not exactly yellow but blue and red, which exploit both earth and sky for their own ends.

Some have described Classicism and Romanticism as a conflict of yellow and green. Classicism, with its roots clearly embedded in Hellenic ideas of proportion, measure, order and light, is, of course, the yellow, and Romanticism, with its emphasis on what is untameable, shadowy, natural, is green. We might also understand the relationship of certain schools of depth psychology as an interplay of green and yellow. Take D.W. Winnicott's many comparisons of the therapeutic situation with mothering activities—this is green. So is Michael Balint's approach to psychoanalysis, as we hear in this passage:

> The analyst must do everything in his power to become, or to behave as, a separate, sharply-contoured object. In other words, he must allow his patients to relate to, or exist with, him as if he were one of the primary substances. This means that he should be willing to carry the patient, not actively but like water carries the swimmer or the earth carries the walker, that is, to be there for the patient, to be used without too much resistance against being used . . . over and above all this, he must be there, must always be there, and must be indestructible—as are water and earth.[169]

Put this green view next to Jung's analytical psychology, which deals in symbol and archetype, and, even more so, to that Jungian offshoot, the archetypal psychology of James Hillman, and the latter seems very yellow indeed.

---

[167] *Pride and Prejudice,* p. 21.

[168] Where do their husbands, Mr Bingley and Mr Darcy, belong in this scheme? I would guess that Bingley, homeless, restless, lively, emotional, quixotic, is a yellow type (mixed with red) and his friend, the man with the vast wooded estates and the ancient pedigree, the man whose temper is unshakeable and whose manner is resolute is more than likely green (with blue). This means the sisters marry their opposites—a highly predictable occurrence.

[169] *The Basic Fault: Therapeutic Aspects of Regression,* p. 167.

I would say that the interplay of green and yellow is behind all the great flowerings of Western civilization. The so-called High Middle Ages, for instance, where the soaring Gothic spire was wedded to the imperturbable centeredness of the rose window; or the Renaissance, where philosophy of a Hellenic stripe was put in service of what Pater called "not the fruit of the experience, but experience itself."[170] At the *fin-de-siècle*, the attraction of yellow to green (and vice versa) was manifested everywhere: in the spread of vegetarianism; in Dress Reform, a movement that advocated healthier, corset-free clothing for women[171] and was an expression of a general freeing-up of the feminine; in Uranism, the first voice of homosexual liberation; in Art Nouveau, where the sinuous, curving, organic forms of plant life dominated canvas, salon and municipal façade. In Britain, in particular, this attraction became a fully fledged love affair.

We should probably pause a moment to look more closely at why and how this was so because many of the preceding references to fictional characters, and those that follow, are drawn from British novels, plays and poetry set during this momentous period in Western history. England has always, of course, had a reputation for being the green land; as Rudyard Kipling put it, "our England is a garden."[172] Historian Wiener explains this ideal of the countryside:

> Until the nineteenth century Britain was still a rural civilisation, whose rulers based themselves in country estates. With the great exception of London, towns played a relatively small part in English history. In Tudor times, visiting Italians were struck by the absence outside the capital of the kind of urban life with which they were familiar. Given the comparative openness of the English upper class, such rural dominance was self-sustaining. From the Middle Ages on, the pull of the country upon successful townsmen was strong and steady: It was a common and feasible ambition for a flourishing merchant to aspire to possession of a country estate. Once in possession, his family would over time merge with the local gentry.[173]

Following in the wake of an industrial revolution that ruffled the appearance of Victorian England came a renewed commitment to the image of the green land, a commitment that bound the arts, politics, education and society together, in a single-minded alliance. It was William Morris's dream—or, at least, one of them, because he also had a dream of London as "small, and white, and clean"[174]—that England, once it had recuperated from the excesses of the

---

[170] *The Renaissance*, p. 152.

[171] Isadora Duncan was a disciple, Elizabeth Kendall informs us in *Where She Danced;* so was the aristocratic Venetian fashion designer, Fortuny.

[172] Martin Wiener, *English Culture and the Decline of the Industrial Spirit, 1850-1980,* p. 58.

[173] Ibid., p. 47.

[174] Ibid., p. 46.

Industrial Revolution, would become again "the fair green garden of Northern Europe";[175] Nature would resume her bearing as a goddess. Echoing Morris, Edward Prior, a spokesman for the Arts and Crafts Movement as it effected architecture, wrote of nature:

> There are Nature's own Textures for us to use. . . . We may borrow from her and show the grain and figure of her works, the ordered roughness of her crystallisations in granite or sandstones, or the veining of her marbles. But it is to be noted that our work in each must take a character from the material . . . as evidence of our delight in texture, we may leave our wood or stone as it comes from the chisel or the saw, to show the fracture the tool has made . . . our plaster may show the impress of the loving hand that laid it, our iron still ring under the hammer that shaped it.[176]

With sculpture, too, like Thornycroft's *The Mower* and Gilbert's *Icarus* referred to earlier, we read of the importance of "naturalness of detail"[177] or of the "naturalistic and fairly detailed way" of rendering the musculature of a human figure in action, "achieving this by careful and detailed modelling, and reflecting this modelling directly in the variegated surface of the bronze."[178]

Composers such as Elgar, Vaughan Williams, Delius, Bridge, Butterworth, and later Bax and Finzi, all celebrated green in pastoral symphonies, rhapsodies on counties, rivers, fens, and "eclogues," tone poems entitled *A Lark Ascending* or *The Banks of Green Willow* or *The Fall of the Leaf* or *On Hearing the First Cuckoo in Spring*. The late Victorian and Edwardian genre painters often depicted the same world, as did poets like Housman in *A Shropshire Lad*. Even Oscar Wilde, a notorious yellow man who provocatively claimed that the business of Art was "to teach Nature her proper place,"[179] pitted the flashy and disappointing theatricalism of yellow against the hardy common sense of green in what he called an etching, *The Sphinx without a Secret*. Here one man confides to another at a restaurant "in the Bois" (that's de Boulogne) how a mystery lady in a yellow brougham proved to be nothing more than a poseuse. The symbolism of yellow and green is in play right from the beginning of the story when the distraught Gerald cries, "Let us go for a drive . . . it is too crowded here. No, not a yellow carriage, any other colour—there, that dark-green one will do."[180]

---

175 Ibid., p. 58.

176 Service, *Edwardian Architecture*, p. 24. Compare this view with that of Prince Albert, who saw the ambition of the age "to conquer Nature to [man's] uses." (Wiener, *English Culture*, p. 34)

177 Benedict Read, *Victorian Sculpture*, p. 301.

178 Ibid., p. 289.

179 Jackson, *The Eighteen Nineties*, p. 75.

180 *Complete Shorter Fiction*, p. 53.

Of course, yellow-green are in a slightly different relationship here compared to earlier examples, for there green was embraced by—for the most part—yellow spirit and imagination and worked into an article of faith, yellow adoring green. In response, green, as Forster said of his milkman Arthur Snatchfold, "burst and flowered and didn't care a damn."[181] For green was, in turn-of-the-century England, not just the landed gentry or *nouveaux riches* with their vast properties but also the men (and women) who ran those properties for them, the gardeners, gamekeepers, ostlers, chauffeurs, in short the working class; and the increase in the value of green led naturally to a new voice for the working man.

It is hard in any discussion of English amors, whatever their color, to avoid the role of class conflict; they cannot be separated, in fact. With yellow and green, the conflict is particularly marked. Yellow is often the far-sighted upper-class man who defies the cultural men's norms by crossing the border from an appreciation of English green into physical passion with one of its tillers. He thus encourages and confirms an impetus usually begun by the green so that both may break out of their confining conditions. Forster's Maurice, for instance, when he discovers that his gamekeeper-lover has not sailed to the Argentine in order to be with him, reflects:

> He had brought out the new man in Alec, and now it was Alec's turn to bring out the hero in him. He knew what the call was, and what his answer must be. They must live outside class, without relations or money; they must work and stick to each other till death. But England belonged to them. That, besides companionship, was their reward. Her air and sky were theirs, not the timorous millions' who own stuffy little boxes, but never their own souls.[182]

English literature and biography of the period contain many similar class-defying romances.

But not only English. Take for example Michel, the philologist hero of Gide's *The Immoralist;* this yellow man shows a marked preference for Moorish shepherd boys as well as French farmworkers, country bumpkins and game poachers. From Dominique Fernandez, we hear of Ludwig II of Bavaria's lovers, who, "rustic and alpine, had for their distant ancestors the shepherds of Virgil's eclogues."[183] In England, however, such pairings were taken as evidence less of exceptional predilections or curious peccadilloes and more of an inevitable compensation for the divisiveness of the class system, in other words, of a revolutionary phenomenon.

Edward Carpenter, one of the most eloquent and revolutionary of the philoso-

---

[181] "Arthur Snatchfold," *The Life to Come and Other Stories,* p. 133.

[182] *Maurice,* pp. 208-209.

[183] *Le rapt de Ganymède,* p. 62. [Author's translation throughout]

pher-spokesmen for the "Urning" temperament in Britain, described his preferred
type of man to the sex researcher Havelock Ellis in the 1880s:

> Now—at the age of 37—my ideal of love is a powerful, strongly built man,
> of my own age or rather younger—preferably of the working class. Though
> having solid sense and character, he need not be specially intellectual. If
> endowed in the latter way, he must not be too glib or refined.[184]

Carpenter had three major erotic relationships with working-class men, one of
whom, George Merrill, was, by touching the visiting E.M. Forster lightly on
the buttocks, to produce a shock of recognition in the latter that led to the creation of *Maurice*. Several of Forster's stories, in fact, feature yellow-green relations between the classes, including *Ansell, Dr. Woolacott, Arthur Snatchfold*
and *The Obelisk*. They are part of Forrest Reid's world, too, as we have seen,
and of the Uranian poet Horatio Forbes Brown. In a poem entitled " 'Bored' at a
London Music," Brown is guest at a salon; the infinitely stiff, polite and dull
proceedings are relieved only by the presence of his hosts' footman. At the end
of every verse, he asserts anew, "I liked their footman, John, the best."[185]

The yellow-green relationship is not always a question of class in the English
fiction we are examining. Sometimes, as in Forster's *The Other Boat* or *The
Life to Come*, it's a question of race. Class is just one of the arenas in which
green-yellow tensions are worked through, but it's an important one; it signifies
the creation of nothing less than a new social order. The yellow's welcoming of
the green as the life principle itself and the green's welcoming of the yellow's
insight as a tool to refine his existence constitute the main action common to all
the arenas. This brings us to the central issue, green-yellow as values and energies circulating between and within individual men.

And also between the masculine figures of a woman's unconscious, as this
dream of a female analysand shows:

> I am with my children in the mountains. We are going to visit a house
> where two men live tending animals. I enter the house. One of the two men
> is an artist. The other has dark hair and a beard mixed with grey, and round
> glasses. He radiates goodness. He tells me he had to leave Yugoslavia, but
> he doesn't know if he can stay here.

The artist and the animal-keeper is a typical union of yellow and green, a marriage of creative imagination and instinct that invariably results in the birth of an
offspring. Not, of course, the biological offspring of the heterosexual union but

---

[184] *Selected Writings*, vol. 1, p. 290.
[185] Timothy D'Arch Smith, *Love in Earnest*, p. 109. A famous heterosexual version of Eros defying class barriers is, of course, D.H. Lawrence's *Lady Chatter-
ley's Lover*.

Peter Pears, 1910-1986 (left) and Benjamin Britten, 1913-1976
(Painting by Kenneth Green, 1943; National Portrait Gallery)

offspring nonetheless. This can take the form of socio-political changes, as we saw, or works of art. In the case of the latter, the collaboration may be either direct—as that between composer Benjamin Britten and tenor Peter Pears, to cite but one famous example—or indirect, where the erotic presence of the partner is enough to stimulate the Muse.[186] The offspring can also appear as the continually evolving or refining experience of male-male relationship, a healing masculine Eros principle in the sense of Forster's famous dictum, "connect—only connect." In the myths and stories we are dealing with, this offspring is frequently symbolized by plants, fruit and especially flowers, those staples of erotic communication. Just as sky and earth combine to produce the flower or fruit, so yellow and green unite in the creation of a dazzling array of blossoms, from the simple and unpretentious to the mysterious and exotic.

What is important here is that a meeting of yellow and green is a prerequisite for any deeply creative relationship between men. Blue and red men, who dominate even the homosexual world, experience an Eros born of their differences; they, too, know the numinosity of the Other. As cultural men, however, their tasks are chiefly preserving, defending and perhaps polishing, the basic creative achievements that green and yellow have won for the culture; they may also provide the means for these achievements to go ahead. For red and blue to become themselves creative, they must connect with the yellow-green axis—and sometimes they do. One interpretation of the purplish flower might be that it is culture itself, a mix of blue and red, that must be constantly renewed through green and yellow union. Culture as Eros?

When green and yellow are allowed room to express themselves in male-male interaction, new possibilities open up for erotic attachment between men. These go far beyond the locker room or bar camaraderie of the business set, the intellectual narcissism of academe and the fast and furious couplings of the homosexual scene in the seventies. Almost a century ago, J.A. Symonds stumbled across this fact on a journey through the Swiss Alps with his daughter. A sympathetic precursor of the Uranian poets, Symonds made a book out of his travel experiences *(Our Life in the Swiss Highlands,* 1892). In the chapter on athletics, he tells of his encounter with alpine gymnasts and of their amazing brotherliness. When he asked their trainer for his comments on the more than fraternal warmth he observed among them, the trainer said simply, "You only learn to love men whose bodies you have touched and handled."[187]

What Symonds perceived and the trainer confirmed was an Eros born of the collaborative struggle by yellow and green for, on the one hand, balance, harmony, beauty of form, and, on the other, unshakable strength, naturalness and an

---

[186] We will see an illustration of indirect collaboration in the next chapter.
[187] D'Arch Smith, *Love in Earnest,* p. 13.

instinctive wisdom. We cannot do better than begin our examination of the two basic configurations of homoerotic relationship with this image of Eros firmly in mind.

Man and Youth

The relationship of man with youth is easily the most discussed kind of homoerotic relationship. With very few exceptions, it demonstrates a green-yellow polarity. The man is usually, but not always, the yellow one, either lunatic or Hellenic type, and the youth a flower boy or gardener. Less often, the older man is prophet-of-the-land or gardener green, and the youth a golden boy or Hellenic-type yellow. We find examples of older-green, younger-yellow in Chiron the centaur and his shining charge, Achilles; in Virgil's Corydon and Alexis; or in fairy tales with Iron Hans and the gold-haired prince; or, more recently, in Elzéard Bouffier and Giono or Zorba the Greek and his English protégé.

Whether the older is yellow or green, the basic nature of the relationship is the same: initiatory. The older man initiates the younger into manhood. From the point of view of an older green man, initiation must move through the senses, the body, to an understanding of the miracles of concrete existence and of the nature of masculinity, its pleasures and perils, its heart and soul. Defined by an older yellow man, initiation is a journey into the lore, the imagery, the traditions, the sacred dimensions of manhood.

Of course, as with the green initiator, the yellow has no other choice than to use the material realm as the testing ground for youth's accession to maturity, but with him, I would say, the exploits have principally a symbolic value. With his green counterpart, it is the immediate experience that counts. (This distinction is something of a simplification, I admit—yellow and green features often appear side by side in the same initiation rites. However, there is always an emphasis in favor of one or the other. Initiation by the green man usually has more of a personal, one-to-one quality about it. With the yellow as initiator, it is more collective, that is, more concentrated on the tradition of the group.) As initiatory relations between a yellow older and green younger man are more frequent—not to mention more celebrated—I shall concentrate on them.

The yellow-man initiator holds the secrets of masculinity in the form of philosophy, song, saying and symbol, which the younger learns to interpret as part of his education. The initiated is green precisely because of his lack of knowledge, his immaturity. His strength lies in innocence, adaptability and physical beauty; these are to a great extent exchanged for other, more adult strengths during the course of the initiation. By "adult," I mean more permanent and culturally useful. At least, it is in this direction that many initiation rites involving homoeroticism tend. Yellow is thus in the service of the prevailing culture, providing it with philosophical coherence via an ever-flowing stream of new recruits.

The most resonant Western mythological model for the initiatory relationship of older-yellow and younger-green is without doubt Apollo and Hyacinthus—although we could point as justifiably to Poseidon and Pelops, Laius and Chrysippus, Hercules and Ioläus, or Hercules and Hylas, to prove our point. The French historian Bernard Sergent sees all of these as expressive of an institutionalized initiatory homosexuality that predated by several centuries the later, so-called decadent boy-love of Plato's Athens.

Few accounts of the exact nature of this institution survive. One of them, appearing in Strabo's *Geography* of the first century B.C., is very telling. Quoting the fourth-century B.C. geographer and ethnologist, Ephorus, on the Cretans, Strabo tells us of a custom whereby a man who had taken a fancy to a youth could go to the boy's family and announce his intention to abduct him. Providing he did this three days or more before the proposed abduction and his rank was equal to the boy's, his announcement would be received by both the youth and his parents as a mark of distinction as only the most courageous boys were considered desirable. Here was an opportunity for the boy to achieve maturity by means of exclusive personal tutelage. Indeed, it was considered a grave dishonor for a youth, especially if he were handsome or of illustrious ancestry, not to have such a mentor, for it meant he would be deprived of an educator whose *arete* or excellence could shape his own. "Only death could erase such an insult," Sergent tells us.[188]

Following a token resistance by his family, the youth was led to his abductor's *andretum* (men's house) along with his age cohorts present at the abduction. There the lover bestowed gifts on him (financed by the lover's friends) and they went off into the bush, still accompanied by the boy's peers,[189] for two months of hunting, feasting and love-making. At the end of this period, they returned to the city and the initiator awarded him three more gifts: military gear, an ox and a goblet. The boy then sacrificed the ox to Zeus and threw a feast for all those who had participated in the bush experience; at this feast he made first use of his goblet.

Sergent notes that the hunt in the bush was homologous in terms of continuity to a campaign in war. In Greek society, the adult warrior and citizen were one and the same. Thus, the gift of military gear underlined the boy's rise in status. The ox, too, showed that he now had the right to make sacrifices, while the gob-

---

[188] *Homosexuality in Greek Myth,* p. 29.

[189] The boy's age cohorts were initiated by virtue of their proximity to the event; in other words, the boy did it not only for himself but also for his close friends who were perhaps not so beautiful or well descended.

let showed his right to participate in a typical civic festival, the banquet. Sergent views the three gifts as a reference to the three functions of ancient Indo-European theology as outlined by Dumézil: kingship and religion (goblet); physical strength and warfare (gear); and productivity, prosperity and health (ox). I feel that the symbolic significance of the gifts underlies the spiritual import of the passage of green youth to cultural man at the hands of the yellow. Could the gifts also be linked, via the three functions, to our color scheme: the goblet to yellow, the ox to green and the military gear (warrior and citizen, or cultural man) to red and blue?

Using this text as a foundation, Sergent builds a convincing argument for regarding the story of Apollo and Hyacinthus as similarly initiatory. Hyacinthus is the youth of good family, of the royal blood of Sparta in fact (Isidore of Seville called him the "puer nobilis"), handsome, courageous; and Apollo his mentor, his erastes (older lover) who instructs him in all that a young man is expected to know in order to assume the mantle of adulthood: archery, music, divination and the exercises of the palaestra. Ovid, Sergent reminds us, even wove hunting exploits into his version of the story. At a certain moment, Hyacinthus dies. Sergent interprets his death as symbolic:

> The antique tradition does not say that Hyacinthus was transformed into the *hyacinthus;* it says that Apollo caused the plant to grow from his body, or that it grew from the blood that flowed from his wound. This second version has a strict parallel with the Narcissus story: It is from the blood of Narcissus, which flows along the banks of the river, that narcissuses grow. Hyacinthus himself will be reborn. Thus the plant does not symbolize a real, biological death but rather a mystical one: It expresses the death of his adolescence.[190]

His death was commemorated annually at the great summer festival held at Amyclae in southern Sparta. During this festival, not only the death but also the apotheosis of Hyacinthus into adult citizen was honored. In fact, the festival was divided into two parts over a three-day period, the first day and a half being dedicated to the death of Hyacinthus, to mourning the hero, to night; and the second to his apotheosis, to praise of Apollo, to midday. "Hyacinthus with the fine head of hair, Apollo brought him back to life," the participants would chant.[191] At the base of the throne of Apollo in Amyclae, Hyacinthus's apotheosis is represented as a transition from beardless to bearded, from eromenos (the youthful beloved) to erastes, from natural man to cultural man, that is, to citizen.

> Hyacinthus is the paradigm of Spartan youth. He expresses the idea that accession to citizenship was like ascension to paradise—a Lacedaemonian way

---

190 Ibid., p. 89.
191 Ibid., p. 88.

of indicating to young people that citizenship is the absolute ideal, an ideological depiction of a relatively prosaic reality.[192]

Sergent goes on to express the deep equivalence between Hyacinthus and Apollo, for

this god is . . . like his pupil defined by his resplendent ephebe's beauty and splendid head of hair; and second, since the erastes-eromenos relationship is temporary, there comes a moment—that of the initiatory ceremony itself—when the eromenos is transformed into an erastes, whereupon Hyacinthus, and all the Spartans who resemble him, play the role that had previously been Apollo's . . . one might even say that after his mystical death Hyacinthus is "reborn as Apollo," if the Greeks, like the Indians, believed in the absorption of one divine (or human) essence by another. The distinction between Hyacinthus and Apollo was always maintained in Sparta. But south of Tarentum, a Spartan colony, there was a tomb of Apollo-Hyacinthus.[193]

In many ways, our view of Hyacinthus as flower boy and Apollo as yellow man (all three types in one) is not disturbed by Sergent's hypothesis. I would, however, question the equation of Apollo and what he teaches with the claims of Spartan citizenship. Why, I would also ask, is Hyacinthus turned into a flower—and just that flower, which, Edith Hamilton informs us,[194] was not the blue or white flower we associate today with the advent of spring, but a crimson poppy or lily-like blossom? What, too, of Apollo's lament over the spilled blood of his lover? Ovid recounts that this lament is preserved in the letters "A I" inscribed on the flower's petals for all to see. And, perhaps this should be the first question, what drew Apollo to Hyacinthus to begin with? And not only Apollo but two wind gods, Boreas and Zephyrus (the jealousy of the latter being sometimes blamed for the death of Hyacinthus), and one mortal, the poet Thamyris?

Sergent doesn't bother with such questions; for him initiation is the central issue. It *is* an issue that is always in the air where a flower boy (and golden boy, too) is concerned and yet it is not enough, I feel, to interpret either the yellow role as simply he who makes it possible or the green role as immature, inferior, something to be gotten over or through. To do so is to commit a common fault in patriarchal thinking, where what is natural is deemed fit only for conquest.

I do not deny the patriarchal basis of such myths as Apollo and Hyacinthus, nor their inevitability. Green youth *is* close to the mother, and it is a struggle for him to win his independence from her. His victory must be proved, he must submit to tests in order to get the confidence and recognition of his elders. But

---

192 Ibid., p. 91.
193 Ibid., pp. 92-93.
194 *Mythology*, p. 88.

what kind of thinking is it that submits the youth to a trial which for any adult male of antiquity would signal ignominious defeat—I mean, the passive role in anal intercourse?

We can accept the explanation of the adults themselves, that in anal intercourse the youth takes in the virtues of his lover in the form of semen (a common explanation in ancient Greece, according to Dover), but isn't there more to it than that? Youth, as Socrates and his companions make clear in *The Symposium* and *Phaedrus*, also confers blessings on the erastes. One, and certainly not the least, of these is inspiration to search for Divine or Sacred Beauty. And we also see with Socrates himself, the real prototype of the Hellenist, that it is the yellow man's special insights—not those of the mere citizen—which penetrate to the green man or flower boy's undiscovered excellence.

In a second volume, Sergent traces the initiatory relationship of green youth and yellow elder through the more familiar terrain of later Athenian and Spartan societies as well as among the Germanic warrior tribes of the fourth and fifth centuries A.D., the Macedonians, the Albanians and even the Celts, citing in the case of the latter the questionable texts of Aristotle and Diodorus of Sicily. The latter's text is colorful, if somewhat outrageous:

> They have pretty wives, but they seldom go to them. Incomprehensible as it may seem, they vastly prefer the immoral embrace of other men. Their custom is to sleep on the ground on wild animal pelts and to frolic with two partners, one on each side. The most surprising thing is that, having no respect for themselves, they surrender their beautiful bodies to other men without resistance and they don't consider this practice shameful. On the contrary, they offer their favors, and when they're not accepted, they consider it an insult.[195]

As for the Albanians, Sergent insists on the initiatory quality of the relationship even when what he describes more closely resembles a comrades-in-arms style of relationship. He quotes Reclus:

> With the Albanians, as with the Serbs and several other ancient peoples, a brotherhood of choice is no less solid than one of blood. Young men who want to become brothers bind themselves to one another with solemn and public oaths; they each open a vein and drink a few drops of each other's blood.[196]

Later, referring to the work of the late nineteenth-century Albanian specialist, Wiegand, Sergent compares the homoerotic relations among young men to that of erastes-eromenos. Each *trim* (soldier) has his *dasure* (beloved). What's more,

---

[195] *L'homosexualité initiatique dans l'Europe ancienne* (Initiatory Homosexuality in Ancient Europe), p. 179. [Author's translation]
[196] Ibid., p. 208.

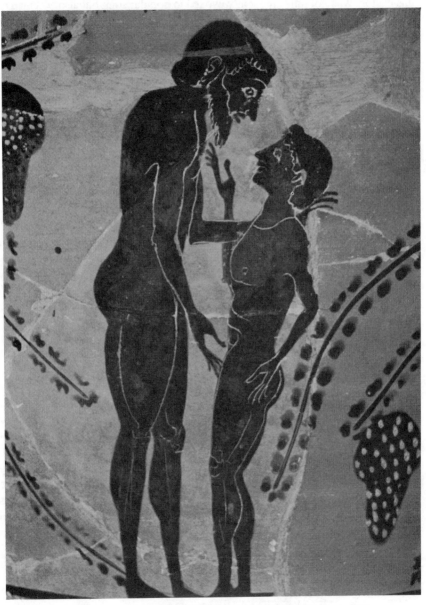

Man and youth, Attic black-figure cup (detail), 6th cent. B.C.
(Museum of Fine Arts, Boston)

this custom was not only frequently evoked in popular song but also accepted by the church. "In Christian tribes, the Church never hesitates giving Communion to young men known to be engaged in pederastic relationships."[197] Because of the relative isolation of the Albanian people, such customs persisted well into the Late Middle Ages. Out of this wealth of material, Sergent concludes that initiatory homosexuality was, in fact, an Indo-European tradition of great antiquity. Only in Rome, it seems, did homosexual relations assume another guise:

> In Greece, homosexual love unites two free men of disparate age. The elder is charged to transmit his virtues to the younger so that one day the latter will be the equal of his teacher and will, in turn, assume the role of erastes and master. Such a phenomenon does not exist in Rome; there, the homosexual relationship occurs between young free men—or even nobles—and their slaves. There is no question of education, of transmitting personal values, or preparing an eromenos to become an erastes. Roman homosexuality is not initiatory.[198]

This Roman brand of homosexuality plays a significant role in defining our second category of green-yellow relationship, but more of that later.

Sergent's theory of an Indo-European institution of initiatory homosexuality can be placed alongside what Carpenter tells us of intermediate types (the half-man half-woman of the berdache) among so-called primitive folk. For example,

> Throughout China and Japan and much of Malaysia, the so-called Bonzes, or Buddhist priests, have youths or boys attached to the service of the temples. Each priest educates a novice to follow him in the ritual, and it is said that the relations between the two are often physically intimate. Francis Xavier, in his letters from Japan (in 1549), mentions this. He says that the Bonzes themselves allowed that this was so, but maintained that it was no sin.[199]

Throughout his study, Carpenter places special emphasis on the religious or spiritual setting for the development of the intermediate youth. Sergent, too, locates the origins of the Japanese tradition of martial homosexuality, the samurai, with the arrival of the Buddhist monks in Japan about 600 A.D. Homosexuality became increasingly popular among the samurai after 1200. Regarded as a more virile love than heterosexual, the love between a warrior and his young lover was thought worthy of the highest honor. For the younger, love took the form of an intense emulation of the older. Listen to the fifteen-year-old Tamanosuke in Ihara's story, *Love Long Concealed,* speaking to his servant:

> "Did not my mother tell you not to deliver love-letters to me if a samurai should send me one? But if you refuse to oblige a man who sends me love-

---

[197] Ibid., p. 209
[198] Ibid., pp. 212-213.
[199] *Selected Writings,* vol. 1, p. 259.

letters, you will act heartlessly. You will be a cruel man. I want to be loved by some great samurai, since that is one of the best things in this life of ours. If no one loves me, I shall hate my beautiful face. . . . I wish you to feel sympathy for pederasty, O Kakubei."[200]

The servant, who has indeed promised the boy's mother to protect him from pederastic advances, replies, "But of course, young master! If everybody were as scrupulous as your mother, such a thing as honourable love between samurai would not exist."[201]

Sergent also refers to initiatory homosexuality among Melanesian peoples, in particular the Big Namba tribe of Malekula Island.

Among them . . . homosexuality was a veritable institution, linked to initiation. Here the essential step was circumcision. When the time for circumcision arrived, the father of the young man set out to find a tutor, a *dubut* or *nembtaremb,* who was well paid with hogs for his services and who enjoyed sexual relations with the novice, the *bau* or *mugh vel.* Homosexual practices were so common . . . that every chief has several eromenoi, and it was said that some men preferred these relations to those they had with their wives. Here a belt of bark had the same significance as military gear in Crete: Until a young man had the right to wear such a belt, he could not have an eromenos. Instead he served as the eromenos of some adult.[202]

Although Sergent does not cite it, much work has been done on initiatory or ritualized homosexuality in Melanesia by the American anthropologist Gilbert Herdt and his colleagues. Widespread in parts of Melanesia, they have found customs similar in purpose to those Sergent describes; in some places, they are still practiced.

Herdt's work with the Sambia is a case in point. With the Sambia, mysterious flute sounds, thought to be the voices of old female hamlet spirits, herald the opening of a long period of initiations. The flutes themselves become the focus of the ceremonies that follow, where boys are beaten, purged, dressed in ceremonial gear and instructed in the mysteries of male power and authority. These are symbolized, on the one hand, by a pair of flutes blown inside one another or by pairs of bachelors; one of the pairs of flutes, the longer and thicker one, is male, the other, thinner and shorter, female. On the other hand, they are symbolized by the erect penis of the bachelors which the boys must suck. The fellatio continues over a period of many years, until the boy passes puberty and assumes the role of bachelor, at which point he becomes the fellated one.[203]

---

[200] Saikaku Ihara, *Comrade Loves of the Samurai,* p. 93.

[201] Ibid.

[202] *Homosexuality in Greek Myth,* p. 41.

[203] Herdt attests to a very special connoisseurship that arose out of these rites. "Sambia have invented an art we could call *semonology:* they are fascinated with

In the Marind-Amin tribe, it was anal sex that was practiced during the initiatory period. It began promiscuously, a veritable orgy, and developed into the typical mentor-protégé relationship. The initiatory ceremonies commemorated the activities of several divinities, including Sosom or Anus-Man who had his penis cut off by the enraged mother of a girl he had attempted to seduce; the old Imo, or Excrement-Woman; and Geb, the moon-man. The last-named lived on the beach as a boy. His body was covered with acorn shell as a result of prolonged underwater fishing. One day, he was discovered by girls whose cries alerted men nearby. They took hold of Geb, scrubbed his body clean of the acorn shell and rubbed his wounds with semen and then they penetrated him. With this, a banana sprouted from his neck (the banana symbolizing the moon in its first or last quarter). They penetrated him a second time, and Geb escaped to the sky where he became the full moon. While this myth accounted to the Marind-Anim for the cyclic mysteries of the moon, it also suggests quite vividly the transformative power of male-male (anal) intercourse whereby the earth boy becomes the sky man. It is thus analogous to Hyacinthus's apotheosis into Apollo.

Among the Orokaiva, a different kind of ritualized homosexuality appears. This takes place between same-sex dance partners who perform together for life at important tribal ceremonies believed

> to bring about a multitude of magicoreligious blessings, from the growth and well-being of the firstborn sons and of taro, to the removal of sorcery spells placed over gardens and hunting grounds, to ensuring a strong sun and good rainfall and thus the invigoration of the whole community.[204]

Schwimmer continues,

> Spirit impersonation invests dancers with awesome and overwhelming power and seductiveness. Impersonation is the form in which the forces of ancestral nature become visible to man. This form is composed of couples, thus expressing the widespread New Guinean view that the universe is made up of dualities, and that whatever is complete has two sides. Between these two sides there must, however, be perfect interdependence. To embody a spirit, a man must have a partner with whom he is perfectly attuned.[205]

Not overt sexuality, but

> homosensuality . . . is the bodily interdependence of the same-sex couple of dancers molded over years of intimate experience with each other. It is

---

the forms, textures, and tastes of semen, which they discuss frequently, like wine tasters. Among boys, a fellated's penis size is not accorded much importance, whereas his seminal fluid, amount of flow, etc., is." (Gilbert Herdt et al., *Ritualized Homosexuality in Melanesia*, p. 210)

[204] Ibid., p. 250.
[205] Ibid., p. 251.

through the close awareness of one's partner that each is able to realize his own godlike identity. Each makes the other into a god.[206]

Schwimmer's example of the Orokaiva more clearly than any other so far expresses the deep spiritual connection, the Self-encounter, that homoerotic bonding can provide. It is composed, too, of a duality between visible nature—the body of the partner—and ancestral—the spirit impersonation—which we could interpret as green-yellow. But the Orokaiva take us again into the realm of comradeship. Where overt homosexuality is concerned, there is only one major exception to the pattern or ritualization or institutionalization in Melanesia: among the East Bay peoples, mutual masturbation and anal coitus is practiced by peers or friends as well as in asymmetrical relationships even in adulthood.

To sum up this phenomenon of ritualized homosexuality in Melanesia, I will cite Herdt's own criteria of definition, namely:

(1) Homosexual practices are usually implemented through male initiation rites, having (2) religious overtones, as well as being (3) constrained by broad cultural rules and social roles, for which the full moral and jural force of a society, or a secret men's society, not only condones but often prescribes sexual intercourse among certain categories of males; and (4) various age-related and kinship taboos define and restrict the nature of this male/male sexual behaviour. Ritualized homosexuality is thus a Melanesian type of institutionalized homosexual activity in the broader sense found elsewhere in the world.[207]

He appends a few more general points to this, specifically: 1) RH (as he abbreviates ritualized homosexuality) is almost exclusively a male phenomenon; 2) partners may not reverse roles; 3) the contacts focus culturally on semen transmission; 4) RH does not involve transvestitism or transsexualism; 5) males engage in contacts first as "insertees" and then as "inserters"; and finally, 6) this relationship often continues after initiation for months or even years.

Lying behind this extraordinary and, until recently, unexplored facet of Melanesian culture is a sense of the inadequacy of the man in the face of the overpowering naturalness of women. According to most Melanesian peoples practicing ritualized homosexuality, men have to be made, women simply are. To compensate for this insufficiency, they promulgate an ideology which mystifies semen as a rare substance conferring virtue, power, strength and wisdom on the youth receiving it. In this way, Melanesian practices resemble the initiatory homosexuality of many of the peoples Sergent discusses. There is a resemblance, too, in the way that women are represented as enemies of semen power. Lindenbaum points out, however, that the attitude to women evinced by such

---

[206] Ibid.
[207] Ibid., p. 6.

societies is one of mystification rather than disparagement. Women are not felt to be contaminating (as they are in societies where power is in the hands of the so-called Big Men who control the wealth of the tribe), but as forces to be resisted through the creation of rites encouraging and honoring adult malehood.

It is significant that societies practicing ritualized homosexuality feature sister-exchange as the preferred marriage arrangement by which one or both partners in the homosexual liaison may be rewarded with the partner's sister in return for services rendered. This exchange serves to strengthen the ties of the participants and thus the cohesiveness of the community at large. The prominence of the brother-sister pair, which I have already touched on in connection with green-yellow relationships, is stressed by Lindenbaum:

> The primordial act of sexual separation is represented in social life by the two men who exchange sisters, giving away that part of themselves that contains a "natural" fertility. . . . Brother and sister seem at times to be treated as a single unit. What happens to one has a consequence for the other. Beardmore (1890) writes, for instance, of a ceremony among Kiwai and Mowat peoples in which a brother leaves the house of his father to reside in the men's house, where men anally copulate with him. At this time, his sister has a V-shaped cut incised above her breasts, a scar she is said to carry for life. This symbolic castration allows her brother to become a fertile being, differentiated from her, and the possessor of their inherited masculinity.[208]

Lindenbaum also remarks that the rites designed to turn boys into men do so by "feminizing" them, making them aware of such womanly qualities as receptivity and submissiveness. But, one wonders, of what use is such knowledge in the training of a warrior (or hunter), a role synonymous, as we noted earlier, with adulthood, citizenship? We know what the boys are supposed to gain through their passive sexual contacts with men, but what, Herdt pointedly demands, do the men gain from it all—besides sexual pleasure? Does the answer have something to do with the mystical marriage of yellow and green forces that each partner, with the aid of the other, comes to see as crucial components of real independence? What they discover together is a creative masculine potency that contains both a striving for sovereignty (yellow) and a capacity to be or to find pleasure in being (green). The relationship also speaks in favor of a balance being struck between Eros and Ares, vital to the sanity of the fighting man, as later examples will clarify.

In our modern Western cultures, initiatory homosexuality is virtually unknown, but it does appear from time to time in dreams.

Twenty-four-year-old Darius, a golden boy, dreamt that an older man whom

---

[208] Ibid., p. 354.

he could not see was penetrating him from behind. They were in an American-style house which Darius associated with his childhood spent in America and his mother's family, in particular, which came from there. A musician and composer, Darius spent a season at music school in America where he met a homosexual man who booked music acts into the local café. This man resembles the dream-lover. In reality, the two did not have sex, though Darius felt drawn toward him. He described the man as more European than American, as having a great knowledge and hunger for Europe. Europe was Darius's father's homeland and we imagined the lover might thus represent Darius's needs to get out of the mother's world and into the father's, the adult male's. Darius also associated American culture with immaturity, vis-à-vis European, and so the dream lover is also pointing in the direction of a cultural adulthood.

The next scene of the dream finds him indeed in a European house, resembling his father's brother's. There, the prominence of the paternal grandmother's bed necessitates another removal and a search for his own house. But, it all begins with the thrust from behind of the dream's erastes figure. Darius had the feeling that the man was using him for his pleasure. I would add, using him as the archetype often needs to use us in order to become conscious. There is no doubt that those same masculine virtues leading to responsible adulthood, with which the Cretans, Albanians, samurai and Melanesians credited semen, are being here implanted in Darius.

We shall now look at the other place in Western culture where initiatory homosexuality has a role to play, that is, in the British public school. Here, as in other societies where initiatory homosexuality is found, the younger partner is green by virtue of his immaturity, his naïveté, his closeness to the mother's world. However, where the yellow man is relatively easy to distinguish in the rites of Melanesia or in the social customs of ancient Greece, by virtue of his magico-religious and philosophical presence, by his emphasis on the mysteries of malehood, he is rather more difficult to define in the public school. Here, he is more often a golden ideal of education, like that propounded by Kipling in his high-flown "If," than an actual person.

From time to time, as we'll see, a yellow man in the tradition of Socrates or the Melanesian mentor does appear in all his radiance, but he is an exceptional figure hearkening back to ancient traditions. On such occasions, he is manifestly not just the teacher or chaplain or coach or prefect—though he may also be one of these. He is a man or senior boy who has an integrity, a passion, a kind of divine inspiration in communicating the light—not the matter—of knowledge and in placing this knowledge in the flow of life. He himself is the man or senior boy one hears called inspiring. "Old boys" speak of him in later life as the one who helped them discover their own vision—some would even say goal—of life.

Simeon Solomon, *Love Amongst the Schoolboys* (detail)
(from Simon Reynolds, *The Vision of Simeon Solomon)*

He is able to accomplish such miracles chiefly because of his erotic attachment
to his charges. We remember what Jung said in his paper on the mother complex
about the frequent coincidence of homosexuality with an ability to teach.[209] In
"The Love Problem of a Student," he fleshes out his idea and adds a scathing
caution:

> A slightly [!] homosexual teacher . . . often owes his brilliant educational
> gifts to his homosexual disposition. The homosexual relation between an
> older and younger man can thus be of advantage to both sides and have a
> lasting value. An indispensable condition for the value of such a relation is
> the stead-fastness of the friendship and their loyalty to it. But only too of-
> ten this condition is lacking. The more homosexual a man is, the more
> prone he is to disloyalty and to the seduction of boys. Even when loyalty
> and true friendship prevail the results may be undesirable for the develop-
> ment of personality. A friendship of this kind naturally involves a special
> cult of feeling, of the feminine element in a man. He becomes gushing,
> soulful, aesthetic, over-sensitive, etc.—in a word, effeminate, and this wom-
> anish behaviour is detrimental to his character.[210]

One wonders to what extent Jung's own experience at the hands of an initiating older friend of the family colored his assessment of the homosexual teacher.
In a letter to Freud (October 1907) he confesses, somewhat shamefacedly, how
his own feelings at the time contained an element of quasi-religious enthusiasm.[211] Such a response would, within the initiatory homosexual framework,
be perfectly normal, not to say archetypal.

In his thorough-going study of British public schools, Jonathan Gathorne-
Hardy speaks candidly of the romantic and sexual possibilities open to the boys
and their masters. The portrait he paints of this hallowed (even today) institution
confirms it as the richest field we know of in Western Europe for cultivating the
initiatory type of yellow-green relationship. Borrowing the words of Faith
Compton Mackenzie, Gathorne-Hardy shows us one of the great public-school
masters, William Johnston (later Cory), who served at Eton in the 1850s as a
brilliant classicist:

> His genius was to make the smallest thing significant to those that had ears
> to hear and minds to respond. It might be a lesson in which he seemed to
> teach twenty things at once, and yet there was no confusion, but a blithe
> leaping from stone to stone in the rippling stream.[212]

Gathorne-Hardy continues in his own words:

---

209 See above, note 3.
210 *Civilization in Transition,* CW 10, par. 220.
211 *The Freud/Jung Letters,* p. 95.
212 *The Old School Tie: The Phenomenon of the English Public School,* p. 186.

To elicit qualities of this sort—of independence, of originality, of unconventionality—requires a great deal more time and attention than is available in the classroom. Cory's lessons, if that is the word, continued in long walks or in endless lazy voyages down the Thames in summer evenings, when he impressed his fascinating personality on the intoxicated and brilliant band of his chosen pupils. And he worked, also, with a skill born of extraordinary understanding. For, as a tutor, it was Cory's intense concern and insight that are so impressive.[213]

D'Arch Smith credits him with an uncanny ability to spot a budding author among his pupils, a few of whom became poets in the Uranian mode. (Several important Uranian poets were schoolmasters as well, notably John Gambril Nicholson and Edmund John, of whom we will hear more later.)

A more recent version of the yellow master can be found in Michael Campbell's school novel, *Lord Dismiss Us* (1967). Both the tutor Ashley and the eccentric chaplain, the Reverend Cyril Starr, belong to the lunatic type, especially Starr. Surrounding himself with the least prepossessing of the younger pupils, nicknamed "Starlings," against whose odor he arms himself with an orange, the aging and cancerous Starr might have been centuries ago "some terrible leader of the Church, and he looked especially right for the Inquisition."[214] He is certainly not above startling the congregation of Weatherhill Chapel with his excoriating lunatic homilies:

"Yes! Yes! Christ is a scorching flame of love! Such love that ravages the heart and soul of those who truly know Him. A love that burns its way to our very innards, reducing to dust and ashes our sackcloth, our pettiness, our pride, our ambition—all the vile balderdash of creed, class, and society—and leaving us naked and alone and free and *joyful* before Him. No, no, no, I tell you! Christ is not a milkmaid! Christ is not a bearded lady! Christ is not even a schoolmaster or a rural dean. Christ . . . is a BURNING FIRE."[215]

We have already heard how head prefect Ralph Lanyon enraptured the fifth former Laurie O'Dell in *The Charioteer*. In Sherriff's play, *Journey's End*, Raleigh's shy but intense admiration, even adoration, of Stanhope, a senior at school, leads him to scheme for a place next to Stanhope in the trenches of the First War. But, there is no need to continue with examples; English literature, theater and cinema tell the story again and again.

It would be a mistake to consider the public school initiation solely a British phenomenon. French playwright Henry de Montherlant's *La ville dont le prince est un enfant* (The City Whose Prince is a Child; 1951) gives us a complex tri-

---

[213] Ibid., p. 187.
[214] *Lord Dismiss Us,* p. 22
[215] Ibid., p. 69

angle of relationships where the Abbé de Pradts, noted for the richness of his nature, vies with a passionately idealistic senior boy for the love of another scruffy "starling."[216] In Richard Meeker's *Better Angel* (1933), the action is transferred to America in the early 1930s. Here, Kurt Gray, the fledgling composer of a suite entitled *On Greenfield Mountain*, has just been appointed music master of a prep school. To his visiting lover, he recounts a typical yellow-green meeting between two of his pupils:

> "There's one youngster here—Clayton's his name. . . . He's got a remarkable talent for the piano; can be a really great performer if all goes well, within and without. He's sixteen, very precocious, very suave and sophisticated in his manner and conversation, but underneath, just an uncertain, unhappy kid. His roommate's a little younger, and a very handsome boy. Clayton got permission to use a practice room after hours. . . . I didn't know about it, and one evening I saw a faint light burning through the drawn curtains, and went up to investigate. When I put the key in the door I heard a great scrambling. It turned out that Clayton had been drilling young Green [!] to dance, naked, to Debussy's 'Clair de Lune.' Green emerged from behind the screen, finally, very red and very much unbuttoned."[217]

But Kurt gets to play the yellow role with Clayton Ford as flower boy when Clayton offers him his confidence on a surprise visit to Kurt's rooms. Kurt explains in true yellow fashion,

> "You're afraid I don't understand, but I do. You're like I was, a good deal . . . set apart from the rest of the fellows here because of your—your taste. They are a healthy happy lot of young animals, but thoughtless, thoughtless. Ford . . . there's a thing in some of us that makes us lonely and unhappy, often. But there's always a compensation if we seek it out, in ourselves, maybe, or in one or two of our friendships. Yours and Donald's [Green's] may be like that. Your music and your love of all beautiful things is another, maybe a more certain one."[218]

Clayton's shy response to Kurt's insights and affirmation is a gift, a replica of Donatello's *David.*

Another example from American literature is even more evocative of what I am trying to illustrate—yellow master as dream-inducer. It comes from Sherwood Anderson's portrait of small-town life, *Winesburg, Ohio* (1919).

> With the boys of his school, Adolph Meyers had walked in the evening or had sat talking until dusk upon the schoolhouse steps in a kind of dream. Here and there went his hands, caressing the shoulders of the boys, playing about the tousled heads. As he talked, his voice became soft and musical.

---

[216] *La ville dont le prince est un enfant,* p. 158.
[217] *Better Angel,* pp. 257-258.
[218] Ibid., p. 274.

There was a caress in that also. In a way, the voice and the hands, the stroking of the shoulders and the touching of the hair was part of the schoolmaster's efforts to carry a dream into the young minds. By the caress that was in his fingers he expressed himself. . . . Under the caress of his hands doubt and disbelief went out of the minds of the boys and they began also to dream.[219]

Accompanying the caresses of this pure lunatic type master are occasional counsels on the order of

"You are destroying yourself. . . . You have the inclination to be alone and to dream and you are afraid of your dreams. You want to be like others in town here. You hear them talk and you try to imitate them."[220]

What is striking about the meeting of green and yellow in the school setting is how rarely green expresses his impressions of yellow, especially as a physical being, and how abundantly yellow effuses over green. This is not only because green youth is notoriously inarticulate—the shy, tongue-tied, blushing pretty boy is a stock figure in school romances—but also because the yellow man, as we have witnessed, is notoriously incorporeal. When green does respond, it is usually to notice the eccentricity and even grotesque qualities of yellow—

The Starlings looked up at the chaplain in fascination. He was an astonishing sight. His head was absurdly impressive: a livid white face with a vast forehead and a thin smooth covering of inky black hair. The central parting was white and faultless. Black eyes twinkled and mocked. The mouth was a wide slit above a square jaw, and it could smile with an infinity of sarcasm and worldliness.[221]

We have to go outside the school setting to the initiations conducted by an older green man for the benefit of his young charge, the yellow man-in-the-making, to get any physical impression of master by pupil. For instance, in Umberto Saba's *Ernesto* (1975), the young title character, an aspiring violinist, takes as his lover a working-class man employed in the same warehouse.

He wore a red kerchief round his head and down to his shoulders to protect his neck from the coarse sacking. He was still young, though it was true he looked tired, and there was something of a gypsy in his features, but thoroughly softened and domesticated.[222]

---

[219] Alistair Sutherland and Patrick Anderson, *Eros: An Anthology of Male Friendship,* p. 310.
[220] Ibid., p. 309.
[221] Campbell, *Lord Dismiss Us,* p. 22.
[222] *Ernesto,* p. 9. Saba's description of the man is remarkably similar to Tom Barber's first sight of Deverell in *Uncle Stephen.* See above, p. 28.

Later the man (he is only ever "the man") asks Ernesto whether he knows what friendship with a man like himself would mean. In reply, Ernesto

> slid his hand from the man's grasp, which had tightened and become damp with sweat, and laid it timidly on the man's leg. He drew his hand up and along till, lightly and as if by chance, it brushed his sex. Then he looked boldly up at the man, a luminous smile on his face.[223]

After sex—Ernesto takes the passive role in anal intercourse of course—the man admonishes Ernesto:

> And don't you think you're the only boy who's ever done what you just did. I asked you for love because I do love you. You're not like other boys, who do it once and never want to see you again. You *are* like an angel to me, and that's another reason I don't want any harm to come your way from this.
> All right, said Ernesto. Then after a pause:
> How many boys do you think have done it?—what I've done today?
> What do you mean, how many boys?
> Well, out of a hundred, say, how many . . . ?
> How do I know? The man laughed uneasily. All I can say is, I never asked a boy who said no.
> This was true; what he did not add was that, guided by a nearly infallible sixth sense, he only ever approached boys who had this particular curiosity in their adolescence.[224]

What these passages typify is the vast difference between the green man as educator-initiator and his yellow counterpart; his blunt tenderness, his insistence on taking things as they are, his "vulgarity" and the importance he gives the physical act of love. Of course, I am making too strict a distinction here, for yellow masters often show themselves remarkably green in their tender and almost maternal support of their protégés—the Abbé de Pradts's solicitude for his gamin Serge, for example, or Kurt Gray's for Clayton Ford. By the same token, green masters, if not Ernesto's man, often create yellowish visions of a world beyond appearances in their lusty hymns to life-in-the-moment that inspire their charges. Zorba is a good example, so is Boyard Manole, the champion of Dionysus in N.D. Cocea's *Le vin de longue vie* (The Wine of Longevity; 1931):

> —Look, boy—his arms fell softly once more to his knees. He leaned slightly toward me, almost resting against my shoulder. And he whispered in my ear: Tst! . . . Listen, boy! . . . Listen to the cricket sing. You would think it was a ray of evening star sizzling deep within the earth . . .
> I listened as if turned to stone. It seemed to me I had been deaf up until now.[225]

---

[223] Ibid., p. 15.
[224] Ibid., p. 26.
[225] *Le vin de longue vie,* pp. 62-63. [Author's translation]

The best, frankest confession of the physical reality of the yellow initiator also falls outside the school romance genre, although it bears many of its features—I mean, Hunt's *Street Lavendar* (discussed earlier in connection with the Golden Boy). Willie's first experience of Joseph Pearson, the man who will become his lover, is as an orator, an impassioned voice condemning the spread of poverty and the capitalistic exploitation of youth in Victorian London. He next encounters him as a customer in the brothel where he works; he cannot see him because he has been blindfolded and tied by his employers belly down on the bed, but he can hear and especially feel him. Joseph is an impassioned lover, too, if invisible. Even at the end of the novel, when Willie has gone to work for Joseph in his hostel for homeless boys, Joseph is heard and felt rather than seen—"Mr Pearson washed my hair himself. He had a lovely touch."[226]

By contrast, the yellow man's effusions over his green lad—for Joseph, Willie is "beautiful," his body, skin "perfect"—place more emphasis on appearance. There is more distance implied in their testimonies of love than with green youth, like Willie, for whom the senses are paramount routes to discovering the Other. For the yellow man the image is sufficient. Even with their countless classical allusions and poetic etiquette, however, yellow effusions over green speak sensually, referring always via the sense of sight to the other senses. Boys are often compared with fruit, flowers, milk, honey, etc. These associations are perfectly in keeping with our understanding of the green youth and his admirer. Public-school boys, like the worldly Willie, are primarily creatures of flesh, hungering for the yellow man's gifts of light—or so, at least, the latter fantasizes.

Themes and motifs other than vegetable do show up in the yellow man's appreciation of the green youth in his keeping; they are just not as important. The boy is sometimes depicted as a prince (in disguise), as a future Galahad, an acolyte, an angel even. The admirer's vocabulary is then studded with light imagery. Cuthbert Wright's choristers, "childish Galahads in passionate red, / Each with his weight of crushing, golden hair,"[227] are a case in point: "From the yellow incense haze, / Beyond a mist of lights, / There springs a face."[228] But these images only serve to heighten the green's sensual appeal by making it seem even more distant, pure and unattainable.

The longing that schoolmasters, tutors, chaplains, expressed, whether they were Uranian or not, was rarely consummated. Distance made a vital contribution to the love dialogue for obvious reasons. Cory was but one famous pedagogue driven from his post by scandal. Allusions like those to Galahad,

---

[226] *Street Lavendar,* p. 327.
[227] D'Arch Smith, *Love in Earnest,* p. 142.
[228] Ibid.

chivalry, Catholic or High Church ritual and Platonic ideals covered, albeit thinly at times, the sexual attraction that was the motive force of the relationship. Writing of the Uranians, D'Arch Smith has suggested that

> There is, of course, a natural physical and mental inferiority inherent in every paederastic relationship; apart from his receptiveness to adult influences which encourages the man to believe he may be of help, the boy's only strength lies in his sexual attraction.[229]

In the library copy of *Love in Earnest*, which I referred to in writing this section, a former reader has put a cross next to the phrase "sexual attraction," corresponding to another cross in the margin beside which he (I presume it is a he) has penciled a very neat "no!" I understand his objection. Even if we are not going to "redeem" sexual attraction by the kind of glossings used in much Uranian poetry, sexual attraction as an "only strength" is not an inconsiderable one: it is, after all, the chief weapon of that charming boy god himself, Eros.

*

I am concentrating on green's impact on yellow, on his service to yellow, because there is little need to comment on yellow's service to green. Yellow's superiority in the intellectual and spiritual sphere is taken for granted in our culture as well as in those of Ancient Greece and modern Melanesia; any interest he takes in the green can only benefit the latter.[230] The pleasure, release, joy, even ecstasy that the green allows the yellow to experience cannot compare in value to what he gives the green—or so runs the argument in favor of yellow's superiority. If, for a moment, we look at sexuality not as an end in itself, but, like religion, as a means to an end—that is, union with the Other—what does the yellow man seek to penetrate in his physical relations with green youth?

I would suggest that with the practice of initiatory homosexuality in ancient European and modern native cultures, the green provides the yellow with an experience of Eros that acts as a kind of compensation for the primary male activities of these cultures that are defensive if not destructive. To put it another way: if a culture grooms men to kill men, and does not provide an outlet for men also

---

[229] Ibid., p. 192.

[230] And green admits it, at least when green is the mystical poet Thomas Traherne, and green lad-yellow master is a metaphor for the aspiring Christian's desire for God's embrace:

His Ganymede! His life! His joy!
Or He comes down to me or takes me up
   That I might be His boy,
And fill, and taste, and give, and drink the cup.
   (Traherne, *Selected Writings*, p. 42)

to love men, then serious imbalance reaching to a profound alienation of men from themselves could be the result. Institutionalized homosexuality attempts to contain this erotic connection ritually.

Modern European culture's warlike activities have been served in a similar way by the ritual vessel which the public schools provided (and probably, to some extent, still provide) in countries like England, as the vast literature of the Great War attests. But it is by no means as definitive a contribution as, for instance, the initiations of the Sambia or Marind-Amin tribes. Men seeking compensation among themselves for the aggression, hostility, frustration and fear perpetrated by male power do so generally with age-mates rather than in older-younger relationships. In other words, the comrades-in-arms relationship is now a more common vessel for the green-yellow dialogue, in life, at least, if not in literature. The image of green youth as Eros is, however, still current in our culture, as a perusal of any anthology of homosexual verse or fiction will show. We will come back to this.

In addition to a god, Eros, the flower boy helps the yellow man contact a semidivine youth, Hyacinthus, in his manifold aspects. One of these is Nature or, rather, the "natural." This is the aspect celebrated by Henry Scott Tuke in his paintings of boys at play. As Symonds wrote to him, "Your own inspiration is derived from Nature's beauty."[231] Tuke's unashamed, glowing Falmouth lads, like Plato's, provided him with a link to Divine Beauty that was not, however, a sky beauty of immaterial forms but "tutto verde, tutto verde, punto giallo."[232] Given the yellow man's distance from a "natural" masculinity, the green youth's service is here invaluable.

Nature also includes the instincts and the senses. The twentieth-century Italian poet, Sandro Penna, sums up the value of the green youth's intimacy with the senses, when he writes, "Perhaps youth alone is ever able to revel in the senses and not repent it."[233] Penna is writing for all older men, but the yellow man in particular, because of his lack of personal connection with body sensuality, feels the contrast most acutely. Many would probably argue that Penna's nostalgia for uninhibited youthful sensuality is a nostalgia for lost youth, that this is the heart of the attraction of yellow age to green youth. I don't deny that in some cases this may be true. Certainly much of the verse singing the praises of youth's irresistible beauty is amply watered with tears for its loss or evanescence but this so-called nostalgia is clearly more than a longing to be young and free again in the corporeal sense. It speaks of a longing for a whole complex of

---

[231] Cooper, *The Life and Work of Henry Scott Tuke*, p. 24.

[232] "All green, all green, with a yellow dot." (Ibid., p. 55) The phrase refers to a method of underpainting that gave Tuke's canvases their special luminosity.

[233] *Tutte le poesie* (The Complete Poetry), p. 239. [Author's translation]

meanings that the green youth carries for the yellow: promise, hope, new beginnings and the capacity for unlimited transformation. He is an invitation to the yellow to believe in the possibility of renewed growth stemming from his own nature.

This is certainly the experience of the old man in Jennifer Johnston's *The Captains and the Kings* (1972) when his loveless life is invaded by the young truant, Diarmid. "A great flower of happiness was growing inside him and as he stood on the top step he began to sing in his old man's voice: 'Voi che sapete . . .' "[234] Gide's academic Michel in *The Immoralist* undergoes a similar transformation when, recovering from a nearly fatal bout of consumption, he is confronted by a Tunisian street boy's physical insouciance:

> The next day, Bachir returned. He sat down as he had before, took out his knife, and in trying to whittle a hard piece of wood stuck the blade into his thumb. I shuddered, but he only laughed, holding up the shiny cut and happily watching the blood run out of it. When he laughed, he showed his brilliant white teeth, then licked the wound with delight; his tongue was pink as a cat's. How healthy he was! That was what beguiled me about him: health. The health of that little body was beautiful.[235]

This confrontation with life lived in the moment guides all Michel's future actions and his life becomes suffused with a strange light.

> Light. A light not so much powerful as plentiful. Even the shadows are full of light. The air itself seems a luminous fluid in which everything steeps— you dive into it, you swim through it. This land of pleasure satisfies without calming desire; indeed, every satisfaction merely exalts it.[236]

Paul Verlaine, in his aptly entitled "Green," writes to his young lover, the mercurial Rimbaud, of a new vitality possessing him which he experiences as a shower, a tempest of green:

> Here are the fruits, flowers, leaves and branches,
> and here is my heart, which beats for you alone . . .
> On your young breast let me lean my head,
> resounding still with your recent kisses,
> let it find calm after the joyful storm,
> and let me sleep a little while you rest.[237]

As the critic Claude Cuénot wrote, "Basically, Rimbaud forced Verlaine to

---

[234] *The Captains and the Kings,* pp. 80-81.
[235] *The Immoralist,* p. 24.
[236] Ibid., p. 158.
[237] *La bonne chanson, Romance sans paroles, Sagesse,* p. 51. [Translation © Decca Records 1990, from a compact disc of Gérard Souzay singing *Airs français]*

become himself,"[238] that is, helped him discover his true nature. (Whether Verlaine might have been more green in fact than Rimbaud who, from some angles, is pure golden boy, does not challenge the archetypal dynamic of yellow man swooning in flower boy's embrace, as presented by the poem.)

In this sense, the green youth is more than an invitation, he is an inspiration to live, a male Muse, as the British poet Ian Young entitled an anthology of homoerotic verse. This Muse is, of course, a relative of Mercurius and the spermatic green of the alchemist's *benedicta viriditas* as well as of the Green Christ in Chagall's Fraumünster windows in Zürich. Green youth is linked directly to Christ in a poem by one of the most prolific Uranian poets, the Reverend E.E. Bradford. It poses the question, "Is Boy-Love Greek?," and answers it with, "Our yearning tenderness for boys like these / Has more in it of Christ than Socrates."[239] Another Uranian, Leonard Green, proposed a vision of Christ that any attractive adolescent might have filled:

> The lustre of crimson roses at dawn is in his cheeks, and in his hair are gleams of blue as in the wings of a swallow. Full and curved and stained with the juice of scarlet poppies are his lips, and his eyes are deep and liquid like the recesses of the ocean. . . . He came leaping to me, comeliness and vigour in his limbs. I drained the poppy from his lips, I crushed his breasts against my own. . . . How shall a man separate God's passion, and the earth's?[240]

Ludicrous as the writing may strike the modern reader, the image of the green youth wedding the earthly to the spiritual is a popular one, an expression of Johannine Christianity, which we shall look at again. For the moment, suffice it to say that the male-Muse image of the green youth, including that of the handsome young red-lipped Christ, represents the possibilities of the green to enlighten and indeed to penetrate the yellow. However, we must take care not to confuse the exalted language of the yellow man with the essentially earthbound virtues of their subjects. The green youths they adore are not golden boys, divine children possessed by longings for eternity. Even though Ganymede is frequently evoked in yellow's hymns to green—especially in Uranian verse where the authors were mostly classicists—he is seldom a disembodied, heaven-abiding cupbearer, but like the following, a very present lad:

> Yes, Ganymede is here among us now
> The gods have lent him for a summer's day.
> Behold the carven beauty of his brow,
> The mystic eyes that gaze so far away,

---

238 Ibid., p. 173. [Author's translation]
239 D'Arch Smith, *Love in Earnest*, p. 3.
240 Ibid., p. 139.

The tender lips, the hyacinth hair of him,
And moulded marvel of his every limb![241]

He is Ganymede mixed with Hyacinthus.

No, if there are any golden boys here, it is among the authors that we find them. Confined by their own strict, hyper-idealistic spiritual terms, they seek the transformation which the "corruptibility" of the green youth permits; they seek to give "body" to the possibility of transformation. It is thus an important aspect of their attraction to the green youth that he is prone to illness, suffering, death and decay. The high mortality rate of the flower boy or *garçon fatal* is finally a testimony to his value as soul-maker; he grounds the yellow man in the inevitability of his own impermanence and forces him to deal with his body as a house for the soul. The twelfth-century Sufi mystic, Sadi, who like so many Muslim poets had an eye for beautiful flower boys, understood the lesson they had to teach in these stark terms:

He who, before he slept or took repose,
  Did roses and the jasmine round him fling;
Revolving time has shed his beauty's rose,
  While from his ashes now the thorns upspring.[242]

More than other men, the yellow man, sensitive to the tragedy of mortality, to the corruptible body (the more beautiful it is, the more tragic), is obliged to find a new form to contain the life that green symbolizes for him. Most frequently, he finds it in art—painting, poetry, dance, music. This way he makes the green youth accessible to all, he makes him timeless without making him eternal. Such a process is at the heart of the Apollo and Hyacinthus myth where god (yellow) falls in love with beautiful youth (green). Though his constant companion and protector, he cannot prevent Hyacinthus's death. In fact, in complicity with his rival, the wind god Zephyrus, he is responsible for it; the discus he hurls is blown by Zephyrus to hit Hyacinthus fatally in the temple. Stricken by the death of his physically superb pupil, he commands a flower to grow from Hyacinthus's blood and on this flower he inscribes his lament.

It is very important that Hyacinthus is not made an eternal companion of the gods, like Ganymede, nor a star in the night sky, but a flower, a perennial flower. Like the Celtic gods who often assume natural forms, the flower represents a *mysterium* impossible to integrate fully. Instead of speaking of Hyacinthus's death then as a return to the mother, as Neumann and others do, we should perhaps view it as a development of *anima vegetativa.*

Sandro Penna seems to be getting at something like this in a poem called "Il

---

[241] J.H. Hallard, "Fettes Cottage," ibid., p. 93.
[242] *The Rose Garden,* p. 167.

Vegetale" (Vegetable Life), where, among the immense green leaves and purplish flower of an incredible plant, the poet is able to connect not only with a real boy left behind but with the very soul of green youth:

> Not for me the myriad
> mutable useless animal forms.
> It is next to you that I can breathe, now that night is falling,
> purple flower unknown: much
> more do you speak to me than their sounds.
>
> You sleep within your immense green leaves,
> purple flower unknown, alive
> like the graceful lad I left
> asleep one day, abandoned in the grass.[243]

With Apollo's lament, we have the model for later elegiac verse celebrating the green youth's ultimate triumph in the artist's hands. The scarlet or purple flower can serve as a symbol for the passing of the youth out of adolescence—this is Sergent's idea—and of the end of the physical side of the erotic relationship. But it also symbolizes the erotic relationship that endures and the transformation of the green youth onto another plane, not heavenly or spiritualized, but sensual—the work of art. As a soulful experience, the work of art provides the only apt complement to the *anima vegetativa* that the green youth serves. Penna's poem, for instance, is as much a "purple flower unknown" as the boy or the desire for the boy which inspires it.

In the art of the West, the elegy for youth is ubiquitous. Sometimes, however, it is the sickly and corruptible aspects of youth that are emphasized rather than his transformative powers. Aschenbach's suspicion of Tadzio's physical frailty gives him an unaccountable frisson of pleasure—and increases his desire rather than diminishing it. So, too, the boys that haunt symbolist canvases with their delicacy—those boys Lorrain has painted in words as "passive beings beloved of perverse gods"[244]—are staring wide-eyed into their own graves. One can imagine the artist himself excited by this dreadful contemplation of the end.

The popularity of Saint Sebastian, emperor's "concubine," as a subject of Western art owes a lot, I feel, to this delight in the death or decline of the green youth. Renaissance painter Guido Reni's voluptuous version of Sebastian's fate stimulated the Japanese author Yukio Mishima's first orgasm, he tells us in *Confessions of a Mask*. So numinous was this image to him that Mishima had himself photographed impersonating "the dolors of a concubine,"[245] with

---

[243] *Tutte le poesie,* p. 57. [Author's translation]
[244] Jullian, *Dreamers of Decadence,* p. 237. [Author's translation]
[245] Tennessee Williams, *In the Winter of Cities,* p. 108.

Sebastian's arrows piercing throat and thigh. The imagery of physical and spiritual ecstasy are wed here much as they are in Bernini's *Teresa* or any of the Baroque and rococo depictions of the mockery and Passion of Christ, which emphasize the whipped flesh, the crown of thorns, the purple robe, the five wounds, over the inner anguish. It is a fetishistic approach to the dying youth, containing for the yellow elements of both sadism and masochism. Even if he stops short of embracing them, it is an approach that brings him up against questions of transformation. Whether he can go farther depends largely on the extent to which his ambivalence can be made conscious.

Sometimes the elegy consists principally of a confession of regret, resignation or hopelessness. A poem by the Uranian John Moray Stuart-Young begins promisingly with the usual floral metaphors,

> A purple passion came to us that day:
> We walked the valley where the lad's-love grows;
> And in the hedges, ruby-red and gay
> A rose hung bleeding, and again a rose.
>
> We talked of love; and he sank on the sward,
> Drawing me nearer in a warm embrace:
> We felt each nerve beat keenly; and toward
> Each other drew, till lips fed on cool face.
>
> "Ah! Love-lies-bleeding!" Soon our moment passed,
> And, softly rising, I said in his ear:
> "How sweet is lad's love!" "But it does not last!"
> He murmured in reply, with sudden tear.[246]

The lad's words prove prophetic, for

> Winter has come, and all the fields are bare;
> I sit alone, and dream of his dear face:
> His look, his voice, his manner, and his air
> Of wistful innocence and childish grace.[247]

Only the poem survives to tell of the lad's love. Similarly, Shakespeare's sixty-third sonnet mourns the evanescence of youth, but at the same time acknowledges a victory: "His beauty shall in these black lines be seen, / And they shall live, and he in them still green."[248] A.E. Housman's final verse in *A Shropshire Lad* expresses the author's self-comforting thoughts that his songs of "light-foot lads" will provide a continuity with succeeding generations of the same:

---

[246] D'Arch Smith, *Love in Earnest,* p. 216.
[247] Ibid.
[248] *The Sonnets,* p. 34.

And fields will yearly bear them
    As light-leaved spring comes on,
And luckless lads will wear them
    When I am dead and gone.[249]

I wish to stress that the victory sung in such poems is not the same as that found in Milton's *Lycidas* or Shelley's *Adonais,* both laments for a beautiful dead green youth. There are certainly similarities, but the victory celebrated by Milton and Shelley is the Christian one of spirit over flesh, sky over earth. For Shakespeare, Housman and many others it is rather the victory of discovering an appropriate language to render timeless a phenomenon of the soul.

The theme of the passing of youth acquired a special poignancy during the First World War. Wrote Wilfred Owen:

War broke: and now the Winter of the world
With perishing great darkness closes in.

. . . .
. . . Rent or furled
Are all Art's ensigns. Verse wails. Now begin
Famines of thought and feeling. Love's wine's thin.[250]

Owen finished this poem, "1914," with a return to the "wild Winter, and the need / Of sowings for new Spring, and blood for seed."[251] This was the blood of green youth.

For Siegfried Sassoon, the war was chiefly "the hell where youth and laughter go."[252] In a long elegiac poem where he honors the memory of a lad killed in action, Sassoon confesses,

My heart is fooled with fancies, being wise;
For fancy is the gleaming of wet flowers
When the hid sun looks forth with golden stare.
Thus, when I find new loveliness to praise,
And things long-known shine out in sudden grace,
Then will I think: "He moves before me now."
So he will never come but in delight,
And, as it was in life, his name shall be,
Wonder awaking in a summer dawn,
And youth, that dying, touched my lips to song.[253]

---

[249] *A Shropshire Lad,* p. 95.

[250] *The Poems of Wilfred Owen,* p. 93.

[251] Ibid.

[252] "Suicide in the Trenches," in I.M. Parsons, ed., *Men Who March Away: Poems of the First World War,* p. 86.

[253] "The Last Meeting," in M. Taylor, *Lads: Love Poetry of the Trenches,* p. 177.

Here again we see the inspirational, Muse-like function of green youth. Green youth as a symbol for the possibilities of life was held up not only in poetry, but also painting and even photography—as the heart-rending anthology of war photos compiled by Laurence Stallings in 1933 demonstrates.[254] However, it was in poetry that the green youth's importance was passionately championed. And chief among the poets of the Great War was undoubtedly Owen.

"It was a Navy boy," he recounts, "so prim, so trim," who gave his heart to Owen in exchange for cigarettes and books—"Who knows my gain!" Owen adds parenthetically. "His head was golden like the oranges / That catch their brightness from Las Palmas sun," "His blouse was all as blue as morning sea, / His face was fresh like dawn above that blue," and "Strong were his silken muscles hiddenly / As under currents where the waters smile."[255] The natural vitality Owen implies by this catalogue of boyish beauty is explicitly acknowledged as he kneels before the brown hands of a young French acolyte:

> Above the crucifix I bent my head:
> The Christ was thin, and cold, and very dead:
> And yet I bowed, yea, kissed—my lips did cling.
> (I kissed the warm live hand that held the thing.)[256]

With "Arms and the Boy," we are thick in the contrast between the hope, promise and sensuality of youth, whose "teeth seem for laughing round an apple,"[257] and the arbitrary destruction of war where the language of lovemaking is perverted into that of rape:

> Let the boy try along this bayonet-blade
> How cold steel is, and keen with hunger of blood;
> Blue with all malice, like a madman's flash;
> And thinly drawn with famishing for flesh.
>
> Lend him to stroke these blind, blunt bullet-leads,
> Which long to nuzzle in the hearts of lads.[258]

Throughout Owen's verse, the sensuous particulars of the adolescent male body—eyes, hands, sides, mouths, backs, chest—bring the poet "by disciplined sublimation at a state of profound pity for those who for such a brief moment possess them";[259] and, I would add, render for us the sense of loss more immediate, more homely.

---

[254] *The First World War: A Photographic History.*
[255] *The Poems of Wilfred Owen,* p. 56.
[256] "Maundy Thursday," ibid., p. 86.
[257] Ibid., p. 131.
[258] Ibid.
[259] Paul Fussell, *The Great War and Modern Memory,* p. 291.

Typical, too, of Owen's verse is a linking of the sacrifice of youth, his fatal wounds like Christ's, with scarlet flowers, especially—appropriately enough for standard-bearers of Eros—roses. Consider, for example, the first version of his famous "Dulce et Decorum Est":

> If you could hear, at every jolt, the blood
> Come gargling from the froth-corrupted lungs,
> And think how, once, his head was like a bud,
> Fresh as a country rose, and keen, and young.[260]

This link is made by many other poets. Louis Golding, speaking to a "Poor driven lad with terror in your eyes,"[261] commiserates: "Your body's like a flower on a snapt stalk."[262] And R.D. Greenway's lad, in "Killed in Action, 1916," was "slight and loose-limbed, blue-eyed, / Swift and straight as a flower in spring."[263] Such images remind us of Uranian verse, like Stuart-Young's "Love-lies-bleeding," but even more of a poem from the *Rubáiyát of Omar Khayyam*, which most of the war poets would have known:

> I sometimes think that never blows so red
> The Rose as where some buried Caesar bled;
> That every Hyacinth the Garden wears
> Dropt in its Lap from some once lovely Head.[264]

We hardly need to point out Apollo and Hyacinthus lurking near this contrast of youth's flower-like beauty with its own murder. The floral bouquets collected round the fallen boy are nowhere so opulent as in a tribute to one of England's darling young men, the self-styled "Neo-Pagan," Rupert Brooke, who was killed early in the war:

> Oh Lovely Lover! No, thou art not fled!
>   From thy red mouth blow poppies glowingly!
> And the wild hyacinth above thy head,
>   Sprang from the tender, dreaming eyes of thee!
>
> Hark! from that thicket, sounds a thrilling thrush;
>   It is thy boy's voice raised aloft to bless—
> All quiv'ring thro' the morning's dewy hush—
>   The rose's dear, unthrifty loveliness.[265]

Such a brazenly erotic tribute could have as easily been written by a Uranian.

---

[260] Ibid., p. 294.

[261] "Joining Up," in Taylor, *Lads,* p. 71.

[262] Ibid., p. 72.

[263] Ibid., p. 139.

[264] Edward Fitzgerald, trans., p. 31.

[265] Peter Austen, "Sonnet to Rupert Brooke," in Taylor, *Lads,* p. 20.

For Owen, the transformation of youth by bullet or bayonet excited no such rapture. His adoration of beautiful youth might connect him with the Uranians, but what he described in "The Parable of the Old Man and the Young" was no initiatory process, only slaughter, senseless slaughter:

> So Abram rose, and clave the wood, and went,
> And took the fire with him, and a knife.
> And as they sojourned both of them together,
> Isaac the first-born spake and said, My Father,
> Behold the preparations, fire and iron,
> But where the lamb, for this burnt-offering?
> Then Abram bound the youth with belts and straps,
> And builded parapets and trenches there,
> And stretched forth the knife to slay his son.
> When lo! an Angel called him out of heaven,
> Saying, Lay not thy hand upon the lad,
> Neither do anything to him, thy son.
> Behold! Caught in a thicket by its horns,
> A Ram. Offer the Ram of Pride instead.
>
> But the old man would not so, but slew his son,
> And half the seed of Europe, one by one.[266]

Here Owen provides as clear a picture as we shall get of the kind of situation that provokes the forming of our second type of green-yellow bond, the brothers- or comrades-in-arms.

Comrades-in-Arms

War is not primarily a theater for the initiatory interaction of yellow master with green pupil. It is rather more appropriate for staging the union of the different but equal forces of the man of vision and the man of the land in the name of a) survival, and b) defeat of a common enemy, usually some representative of patriarchal war-mongering. Of course, war *can* be a theater for the development of the unequal relationship of man with boy into the full equality of comrades-in-arms, as we will see with Ursula Zilinsky's Second World War novel, *Middle Ground.* Owen himself, Fussell says, demonstrated this development:

> If the boys of Owen's early imagination begin as interesting "lads," ripe for kissing, they end as his "men" in France, types not just of St. Sebastian but of the perpetually sacrificed Christ. . . . The tradition of Victorian homoeroticism teaches him how to notice boys; the war, his talent, and his instinct of honor teach him what to make of them.[267]

---

[266] *The Poems of Wilfred Owen,* p. 151.
[267] *The Great War and Modern Memory,* pp. 286-287.

Two Hearts That Beat As One
(Life in the British Forces, East Kent Mounted Rifles, 1921)

In "Futility," the corpse addressed is no longer a beautiful boy's, but a fallen man's:

Move him into the sun—
Gently its touch awoke him once,
At home, whispering of fields half-sown.
Always it woke him, even in France,
Until this morning and this snow.
If anything might rouse him now
The kind old sun will know.[268]

As with the yellow master and his still-green pupil, it falls to the yellow half of the comrades-in-arms couple to honor and celebrate the unsung values of the green. Here, these are not synonymous with youth, innocence, playful Eros—at least, not primarily—but with those of rich Mother Earth herself. It is the gardener type of green man of whom the yellow man sings, and if Aldington's view that "Each wound on the breast of earth, / Of Demeter, our Mother"[269] wounds us also, the reverse is just as true for many of the war poets. Their victim is invariably green and his destruction is a blow struck against the Great Mother herself, against the life principle.

The gardener is identified with the earth he tends, but it is only in collaboration with the yellow—either Hellenic or lunatic—that the fruits of his labors are finally brought in. This collaboration is marked, as I've said, by equality, by solidarity, by an Eros of "only connect" that defies division. Lines of class, creed, color, country are overridden by the intensity of the drive to mate. Matehood indeed became an institution stronger than marriage in the trenches of the First World War; even today, Englishmen, regardless of their sexual inclinations, will speak fondly of their "mates."

The collaboration of green and yellow mates produced a type of symbolic gardening, the fruit of which was a thrilling, resounding affirmation of life in the raw. Such an affirmation clearly established the yellow-green comradeship as revolutionary in the face of the general's aims. "War—and gardening!" Siegfried Sassoon tells us, "Those are the poles."[270] The Italian poet Ungaretti put it very clearly, too, in "Watch," written during the Cima Quattro campaign of December 1915:

A whole night through
thrown down beside
a butchered comrade

---

[268] *The Poems of Wilfred Owen,* p. 135.
[269] "In the Trenches," in Parsons, *Men Who March Away,* p. 106.
[270] Fussell, *The Great War and Modern Memory,* p. 234.

with his clenched teeth
turned to the full moon
and the clutching
of his hands
thrust
into my silence
I have written
letters full of love

Never have I
clung
so fast to life[271]

"Never have I clung so fast to life" could be the motto of the green-yellow comrades' experiment in survival. In this, they are different from their counterparts in the man-youth relationship more by quality than quantity. There's more roughness, more adventure, more risk, more of the heroic in their relationship (though this is not always true, as Gide's Michel proves).

Many of the Uranian writers, Hellenic types mostly, sang of the loss of the flower boy, transcribing his youth and beauty into the enduring sensuality of the erotic image. But the yellow elegist of the comrades-in-arms pair testifies to the persistent, one might say stubborn, possessive, clinging nature of life, of the urge to go on being, creating, even, or perhaps especially, when confronted with imminent annihilation, whether from mortar shell, madness, despair or disease. This is the green comrade's legacy to the yellow; transcribed, it becomes the latter's legacy to his culture, particularly to the men of his culture. Their love for one another, itself an expression of indomitable life, is the vessel or plot (in the sense of a garden plot) where the hardiness of life is tested.

Ungaretti's poem, like so many others of the time, challenges and refines the notion of immortal life and so leads to a new spiritual orientation in which earthly existence is accorded a higher value. Such poems belong to a long line of lyrical attempts to fathom the meaning of a comrade's death, to understand the inextricability of the life-death dyad, but also to insist upon its cyclical nature and to point out ceaselessly the new life that follows death. The green comrade, in his splendid mortality, mirrors the yellow's own life-death struggles.

In the decades before the First World War, Tennyson's sometimes unbearably tender epic of lamentation for his lost friend Hallam, *In Memoriam,* and poems such as Walt Whitman's "Vigil Strange I Kept on the Fields one Night" or "As Toilsome I Wander'd Virginia's Woods"—both of them, in fact, war poems—set the tone for their successors. Voicing doubt for the reception of his lullabies of pain, Tennyson envisages a man stumbling upon them in a book stall,

---

[271] *Selected Poems,* p. 28.

And passing, turn the page that tells
A grief, then changed to something else,
Sung by a long-forgotten mind.

But what of that? My darken'd ways
Shall ring with music all the same;
To breathe my loss is more than fame,
To utter love more sweet than praise.[272]

Whitman himself stumbles upon evidence of the tenacious love of comrades:

As toilsome I wander'd Virginia's woods,
To the music of rustling leaves kick'd by my feet, (for 'twas autumn,)
I mark'd at the foot of a tree the grave of a soldier;
Mortally wounded he and buried on the retreat, (easily
          all could I understand,)
The halt of a mid-day hour, when up! no time to lose—
          yet this sign left,
On a tablet scrawl'd and nail'd on the tree by the grave,
Bold, cautious, true, and my loving comrade.[273]

Seasons pass, the scenes of his life change, and still the words of tribute, "Bold, cautious, true, and my loving comrade," return to haunt the poet.

It is hardly an accident that autumn woods provide the setting for Whitman's discovery, for among these the gardener resides. Here must the yellow man look if he is to get to the heart of him. For the Great War poet, the battlefield is the distant echo of another kind of field, one meant for farming.

This ploughman dead in battle slept out of doors
Many a frozen night, and merrily
Answered staid drinkers, good bedmen, and all bores:
"At Mrs. Greenland's Hawthorn Bush," said he,
"I slept." None knew which bush. Above the town,
Beyond "The Drover", a hundred spot the down
In Wiltshire. And where now at least he sleeps
More sound in France—that, too, he secret keeps.[274]

Surviving the loss of such a one is the question that haunts E. Hilton Young:

This was the way that, when the war was over,
we were to pass together. You, its lover,
would make me love your land, you said, no less,
its shining levels and their loneliness,
the reedy windings of the silent stream,
your boyhood's playmate, and your childhood's dream.
The war is over now: and we can pass

[272] *In Memoriam, Maud and Other Poems,* pp. 114-115.
[273] Walt Whitman, *The Complete Poems,* p. 332.

this way together. Every blade of grass
is you: you are the ripples on the river:
you are the breeze in which they leap and quiver.
I find you in the evening shadows falling
athwart the fen, you in the wildfowl calling:
and all the immanent vision cannot save
my thoughts from wandering to your unknown grave.[275]

How to recover life when hope has retreated, "bleeding and forlorn"?[276] The
concerns of the green comrade, as imagined by W.W. Gibson, are much more
modest in expression—less exalted anyway—but no less poignant when heard
amid the rage of battle:

And all I think of, as I face the foe
    And take my lucky chance of being shot,
Is this—that if I'm hit, I'll never know
    Till Doomsday if the old cow died or not.[277]

This is Demeter herself whose survival depends on the survival of what the
green man represents.

With images of cows, fields, brooks and trees belong, naturally, flowers. We
have noted the importance of floral symbolism in capturing the essence of our
first type of green-yellow relationship. In the comrades-in-arms relationship,
where the green man is the man of the land, flowers play an important role in
describing yellow's feelings about the green, but they have perhaps fewer nu-
ances of meaning; they are more emblematic than symbolic. Perhaps this has
something to do with the fact that the green-man gardener type personifies the
enduring aspect of nature, and flowers rather its fragile and fleeting side. They
can, of course, represent the inexpressible life force of the green as well as the
flowering of yellow's understanding and appreciation of the green man's language and ways.

As with flower boys mourned by their melancholy mentors, red and purplish
flowers dominate the garden of the yellow man's poetic tributes to the man of
the land. Taking his cue perhaps from Tennyson's *In Memoriam,* where the author sees rising from Hallam's ashes "the violet of his native land," Ivor Gurney
calls for help in covering over "that red wet / Thing I must somehow forget," his
dead lover, "With violets of pride / Purple from Severn side."[278] H.P. Dixon in
the "lilac-scented air" after Sunday vespers, walks thinking of "one / Who went

---

[274] Edward Thomas, "A Private," in Parsons, *Men Who March Away,* p. 148.

[275] "Return," in Taylor, *Lads,* p. 205.

[276] Murray McClymont, "To a Fallen Comrade," ibid., p. 179.

[277] "The Question," in Parsons, *Men Who March Away,* p. 82.

[278] "To His Love," ibid., p. 153.

a-soldiering."[279] For the Canadian war poet, F.O. Call, much admired by the so-called Georgian poets of England, the "poppies blazing red" which now dot the graveyards of fallen soldiers instead of "waving wheatfields"[280] are understood patriotically as symbols of sacrifice—a Christ-like sacrifice, so that others might live and the land might bloom again, in other words a typical green sacrifice. By far the most popular, though certainly not the best war poem, also by a Canadian, Lieutenant John McCrae, makes similar allusions to the glowing poppy in its formerly pastoral setting:

> In Flanders fields the poppies blow
> Between the crosses, row on row,
>   That mark our place; and in the sky
>   The larks, still bravely singing, fly
> Scarce heard amid the guns below.
>
> We are the Dead. Short days ago
> We lived, felt dawn, saw sunset glow,
>   Loved and were loved, and now we lie
>   In Flanders fields.[281]

The more collective view presented by McCrae does not, however, diminish either the tragedy of war or the oppositional force provided by a tacit homoeros.

With this red-purple floral imagery we are back in the company of Apollo and Hyacinthus once more. It is perhaps the place here to remark that very often the relationship of yellow master to his green pupil matures into a comrades-in-arms relationship. Although the various versions of the myth agree about Apollo's role as tutor and his superiority as a god, some, for example Jean Broc in his neoclassical painting *The Death of Hyacinth* (above, page 54), reduce the disparity in age and accomplishment in order to emphasize the comradeship aspects. Apollo is then depicted as Hyacinthus's age-mate—and as the very model of ephebic beauty he has a right to the role—while Hyacinthus's beauty and receptivity prove a worthy equal to Apollo's gifts. The Theban band, that renowned battalion composed exclusively of pairs of lovers, as well as the more civilian pairings of later Athens, reflect, according to Dover, a similar blending of teacher-pupil and comrades-in-arms relationships.

Overlappings—one might say hybrids—can also be found among the samurai and in some Melanesian tribes where even if the sexual relations between partners cease, the erotic connection remains alive. Sergent recounts that the young Cretan abducted to the bush by his mentor held thereafter a favored position in

[279] "In Memoriam," on the record *Songs by Finzi and His Friends.*
[280] *In a Belgian Garden and Other Poems,* p. 13.
[281] Fussell, *The Great War and Modern Memory,* p. 249.

his society by virtue of his seduction: he was *kleinos* (a famous one). By the same token, many of the comradeships we will now look at contain initiatory elements whereby one or both partners are enabled to develop, or even to change status.

The term "comrades-in-arms" implies battle, and even if all the pairs of lovers referred to here are not engaged in battle on the scale of the Great War, a shoulder-to-shoulder front against a common enemy is an unmistakable feature of their relationship. The most celebrated examples of such pairs are also among the oldest; Gilgamesh and Enkidu, Achilles and Patroclus, Damian and Pythias, Harmodius and Aristogeiton, Orestes and Pylades, David and Jonathan. All of these couples demonstrated how homoerotic love could subdue tyranny or abuse of power. Of these, Achilles and Patroclus and David and Jonathan have become synonymous with intense male-male friendships. For instance in *John Halifax, Gentleman*, Mrs. Craik's mid-nineteenth-century moral tale for young people, the crippled, bookish Phineas, son of a Quaker merchant, depicts his relationship to the muscular-limbed working boy, John Halifax:

> We had the garden all to ourselves—we, Jonathan and his new-found David.
> I did not "fall upon his neck," like the princely Hebrew, to whom I have likened myself, but whom, alas! I resembled in nothing save my loving. But I grasped his hand, for the first time, and looking up at him, as he stood thoughtfully by me, whispered, "that I was very glad."
> "Thank you—so am I," said he, in a low tone. Then all his old manner returned; he threw his battered cap high up in the air, and shouted out, "Hurrah!"—a thorough boy.[282]

Similarly, Ronald Firbank's queerly comic novella, *Valmouth* (1919), demonstrates the persistence of Achilles and Patroclus's friendship in inspiring imitation. Thetis Tooke, enamored of the absent Dick Thoroughfare, remembers the day

> he had told her of his ship—the *Sesostris*—and of his middy-chum, Jack Whorwood, who was not much over fifteen, and the youngest hand on board. "That little lad," he had said, with a peculiar smile that revealed his regular pointed teeth, "that little lad, upon a cruise, is, to me, what Patroclus was to Achilles, and even more."[283]

Firbank clearly took Achilles as the older and Patroclus as the younger. When his Patroclus finally appears in the novel, with his romantical curls and rose-mauve lips, he is decked out like a caricature of the flower-boy:

---

[282] Dinah Maria Mulock, *John Halifax, Gentleman*, p. 18.
[283] *Valmouth*, p. 22. There is another green type in *Valmouth*, the dashing dairy-man David Tooke referred to as a "crazy Corydon" and an "inverted flower," sensible only to the claims of hound, cattle and timber.

He had a suit of summer mufti, and a broad-brimmed blue beaver hat looped with leaves broken from the hedgerows in the lanes, and a Leander scarf tucked full of flowers: loosestrife, meadowrue, orchis, ragged-robin.[284]

There is some argument among Greek scholars as to which, Achilles or Patroclus, was erastes and which eromenos, although a bowl of 500 B.C. showing a beardless Achilles binding the wounds of a bearded Patroclus (below, page 128) suggests that the latter was the initiator. Whatever age difference actually existed between them, they have come down to us as loving comrades fighting the battle for Troy. Achilles is given the yellow role (golden boy) in this campaign and Patroclus the green (gardener). The bowl's view of Patroclus' exposed genitals and body hair points, I feel, to his greenness as much as to his age. Besides his obvious devotion, even reverence, for the green depicted by the bowl as his bandaging attempts, Achilles' gifts as an elegist lamenting the death of his green comrade would mark him as yellow. In Homer's *Iliad,* of which Beinecke says, "the main motive is the love of Achilles for Patroclus,"[285] his mourning places him on a par with many later bereaved yellow men clamoring for enlightenment and restitution:

A black cloud of grief enwrapped Achilles, and with both hands he took dark dust and poured it over his head and defiled his comely face, and on his fragrant doublet black ashes fell. And himself in the dust lay mighty and mightily fallen, and with his own hands tore and marred his hair. . . . And Antilochos . . . wailed and shed tears, holding Achilles' hands while he groaned in his noble heart, for he feared lest he should cleave his throat with the sword.[286]

With David and Jonathan, the roles of yellow and green undergo mutation. David begins his extraordinary career as green man, both flower boy and man-of-the-land, for he is a shepherd. As the Bible tells us, this green youth captivated Jonathan, the king's son (a role suggesting yellow):

When he had finished speaking to Saul, the soul of Jonathan was knit to the soul of David and Jonathan loved him as his own soul. . . . Then Jonathan made a covenant with David, because he loved him as his own soul. And Jonathan stripped himself of the robe that was upon him, and gave it to David, and his armour, and even his sword and his bow and his girdle.[287]

Jonathan in this way prepares David for his accession to the yellow role of kingship which he, undone by his love for David, is only too willing to hand

---

284 Ibid., p. 95.
285 Edward Carpenter, ed. *Ioläus: An Anthology of Friendship,* p. 68.
286 *The Iliad,* p. 259.
287 1 Samuel 18: 1-4.

over. In Gide's drama, *Saül*, we find Jonathan removing the heavy crown his father has placed on his head and passing it to David with the phrase, "How well it suits you!"[288] Jonathan is as one possessed by the green-man archetype as he divests himself of his purple finery:

> Ah! Daoud! I would like to toss these bits of royalty to the ground. . . . I would like to stretch out on the earth and sleep. . . . Ah! Would that I were like you, a goatherd, naked under a ewe's fleece—in the open air.—How beautiful you are, David!—I would like to walk with you on the mountain. You would clear my path of every stone. At noon we would bathe our tired feet in fresh water, then we would sleep in the vines. You would sing and I would embellish my love for you.[289]

David is convinced not by his argument but by Jonathan's beauty clothed only in a simple undertunic, and accepts his cast-off royalty vowing to become his protector, his consolation. As he takes on the yellow role, Jonathan slips quite naturally from golden boy to flower boy.

The common enemy both David and Jonathan face is the kind of power represented by the scheming, unpredictable, violent king, Saul. For Jonathan that power means something stifling his natural inclinations, his yearning for the green life, the verdant valley where "delicate flower," as David calls him, he might find protection from "a sun too ardent."[290] It is put even more directly in Marc-Antoine Charpentier's 1698 opera, *David et Jonathan*, where the latter equates nature with love and pits it against duty: "I owe everything to Saul; but nature, too, / Alas! strikes my heart with a thousand mortal blows. / Will I never bring beauty and love together?"[291]

For David, Saul's power is the obstacle preventing him from realizing his innate royalty, his yellow nature. It is only with the deaths of Saul and Jonathan, the latter obliged to fight on his father's side against David, that David claims the yellow role fully and becomes, in the tradition of yellow men, the elegist: "I am distressed for you, my brother Jonathan; very pleasant you have been to me; your love was wonderful, passing the love of women."[292]

---

[288] *Saül*, p. 92. [Author's translation]

[289] Ibid., p. 93.

[290] Ibid.

[291] Dominique Fernandez, *Le rapt de Ganymède*, p. 205. [Author's translation]

[292] 2 Sam. 1: 26. David as he appears in Timothy Findley's novel, *The Wars* (1977), is the handsome Captain Taffler who seeks not a Jonathan to love, but a Goliath to defeat. He complains, "All you get in this war [the Great War] . . . is one little David against another. . . . Just a bunch of stone-throwers." (p. 35) Later the overprotected hero-narrator watches Taffler through a peephole in the wall of a bordello room, being ridden like a horse by a mute, white-blond Swede, the bordello's bouncer, and concludes that here at least he has met his Goliath.

David calls Jonathan his brother, an appellation that belongs very much to the comrades-in-arms relationship. It suggests not only the closeness, the intimacy of the relationship, but also the equality of the green and yellow values. Erich Neumann has examined certain myths of twin brothers, notably that of the Dioscuri (Castor and Pollux), where one of the twins is mortal and the other divine.[293] These he equates with chthonic and spiritual which I would interpret as the extremes of green and yellow, but for Neumann these do not have equal weight: the earthly is both destructive and self-destroying and must be transcended (or assimilated). This is not a surprising conclusion for Neumann to come to if we remember that on several occasions he described the chthonic masculine as a vassal in the "lower" world of the Great Mother where consciousness languishes, a hapless prisoner.

Inspired by David's testimony of friendship with Jonathan in 2 Samuel 1, Peter Abelard fashioned a beautiful *planctus* (lament) where he elaborates on the meaning of brotherhood:

> More than a brother to me, Jonathan,
> One in soul with me . . .
> How could I have taken such evil advice
> And not stood by your side in battle?
> How gladly would I die
> And be buried with you!
> Since love may do nothing greater than this,
> And since to live after you
> Is to die forever:
> Half a soul
> Is not enough for life.[294]

What Abelard expresses here is a kind of mystical marriage, a soul-knitting in which the loss of one's more-than-brother, more-than-equal is the equivalent of losing a supraordinate value without which life is meaningless. Whether the value lost happens to be green or yellow does not affect the picture except in its details. Such a union as Abelard intimates resembles that implied by Aristophanes in his *Symposium* speech where the halves of a former whole yearn desperately for reconnection. It also bears a relation to the union described in St. John's version of the Passion. Christ on the cross presents Mary, his mother, to the beloved disciple as the latter's own mother, and John to Mary as her son.

I do not want to push this point for Christ is, of course, both yellow and green as well as blue and red. Taking Chagall's Green Christ as support, however, I could argue that Christ's relationship to John is that of green comrade to

---

[293] *The Origins and History of Consciousness,* pp. 180-181.
[294] John Boswell, *Christianity, Social Tolerance and Homosexuality,* p. 238.

yellow, of man of the land (even flower boy) to lunatic man of vision. I am referring not only to the gift of his mother—which a yellow man could never offer
a green—not only to John's status as beloved or to his place on Christ's bosom
at the Last Supper, but also to John's ecstatic yellow visions of the kingdom-to-
come mentioned earlier. Christ's sacrifice, too, his dismemberment and reconsti-
tution, is again typical of green men before (Osiris, Attis, Adonis, Balder) and
after (the victims of the Great War mourned by Owen, for example), pointing as
it does to the archetypal longing for renewal and a refusal of the void.

The tender and ecstatic or mystical sides of Christ's relationship to John has
been captured by numerous artists as different as Bellini, Grünewald, Delacroix
and Ernst Alt. In so many of these images we find John dressed in red, partly, we
assume, as a declaration of his love and passion for Christ, and partly as a sign
of his identification with Christ's wounds, with that greater Passion. In a sense
their erotic connection is sealed in those wounds by that other Passion. We
should not forget either that legend says the rose, flower of love, first grew from
the blood of Christ dripping from the cross; this is yet another variation on an
image we have seen several times already, the birth of Eros out of an encounter
of yellow and green.

Julien Green's play *Sud* shows a young man named Ian (read: John) Wiczew-
ski provoking the green man he loves (a plantation owner) but cannot confide in
to a duel where he allows himself to be killed. Horrified, his host, an older man
and a kind of mentor, chastises the assassin with these impassioned words:

> If Jesus were here, we would make him weep with shame, yes with shame,
> before the perpetual failure of his Word. It's he you have struck with your
> cursed weapon and it's the blood of Christ that has flowed over the face of
> this man. It is always Christ's blood that flows when a man is killed.[295]

Ian's blood creates an erotic tie between Ian and Christ as well as between
him and his beloved killer. It is interesting that Ian is the yellow man in *Sud* and
that he can only join with the green through the kind of sacrifice usually reserved
for the man of the land.

Ian's death is a comment on the failure of society—a bellicose Christian society—to allow merger of the halves through any other means. The death of a yellow man in such circumstances is like the snuffing out of the last bit of candle-
light in a dim room; with him goes all hope for a new day. Even if the green
survives, as he does in Green's drama, his future growth is so tied to collaboration with the yellow that it is only just survival—both for him and the culture
he serves.

Still within the Christian tradition are the legendary medieval pair, Amis and

---

[295] *Sud*, p. 188. [Author's translation]

Amile, exemplary comrades-in-arms whom we cannot distinguish as we have our other comrades, one as green, the other yellow. Their history, however, demonstrates a continuous interplay of green and yellow values, which I would here delineate as a tender, nurturing care for the earthly well-being of each other combined with a quest for moral truth and justice.

Born on the same night of different parents, Amis and Amile are identical, *Doppelgänger,* a circumstance that proves very useful in the many knightly trials they face together. It also maximizes the brotherly nature of their devotion to each other and minimizes the sexual, which, always implicit if not explicit in Greek and Middle-Eastern legends of friendship, has given way under Christian pressure to a more spiritualized passion. Passion it nonetheless is and it is given expression in acts of self-sacrifice and devotion rivaling the Greeks.

Amis and Amile's ardent commitment to one another is symbolized by two identical bejeweled cups bestowed on them by the Pope at their joint christening in Rome. These cups suggest, of course, the Grail, Christ's wounds, His blood, and the Eros both sacred and profane sealed in that blood. Amis's cup serves to identify him to his long-separated friend when he shows up at Amile's palace as a beggar, outcast and gravely ill with leprosy: it is a reminder of their mutual pledge of containment. Amile takes his friend into his bed—in spite of Amis's illness and his own wife—and ministers to him vigilantly. The angel of healing, Raphael (in some versions of the tale, Gabriel), appears and informs them that Amis can be healed only if Amile smears the body of his friend with the blood of his children. Both are horrified with the terms, but Amile complies and Amis is healed. For his devotion, Amile is rewarded with the resurrection of his children who ever after sport a thin red necklace where their wounds were. When Amis and Amile eventually die together in battle, they are laid to rest in coffins near one another—not near enough, however, for the coffins leap the distance between them so that the heroes will not be separated at any level, even that of putrefaction. Some versions of the tale even speak of rosebushes entwining their branches above the coffins.

This story inspired hundreds of imitations. One of the most interesting is a Sicilian tale which Andrew Lang included in his fairy-tale series. Its world is definitely not the Middle-European world of patristic Christianity to which the love of Amis and Amile acts as compensation, but that of Mediterranean matriarchy. Its ruler is a widowed queen, mistress of vast estates and ripe cornfields. Reluctantly, she prepares to send off her darling eighteen-year-old son to the shrine of St. James (brother of John, incidentally) in order to fulfill a promise made to him at the boy's birth. (It was through James's intercession that the birth was made possible.) This is not the place to analyze the details of this engagement of matriarchal pre-Christian forces with patriarchal and Christian—important as it is for the understanding of the tale. Rather I wish to focus on the invaluable advice mother gives son prior to his journey:

> "If you come across a young man who pleases you, beg him to accompany you. . . . Cut one of these apples into two unequal parts, and ask him to take one. If he takes the larger bit, then part from him, for he is no true friend to you. But, if he takes the smaller bit, treat him as your brother, and share with him all you have."[296]

Crudely put, the test proposed by the queen is meant to determine whether or not the prospective friend is an egotist. Humility and deference are universally acknowledged signs of a true friend and what makes them so is their clear admission that there is something greater than the ego's needs; they are signs of a consciousness of a higher power, of the existence of a true being, as Plato said in *Phaedrus,* or, in analytical psychology's terms, of Self. This power is projected onto the friend. That such a projection might serve as the archetypal dynamic working in same-sex relationships is the same idea put forward by Stevens.[297]

The apples are clearly symbols of totality, being spheres, as well as of earthly desires and Eros—they are after all used to find a companion, more than that, a soul-mate who will recompense the hero for his travails in the world of the fathers and also provide him with the occasion to exercise his heroism in the service of relatedness. That mother has this knowledge of Eros accords well with one ancient tradition that sees Eros as the son of the Great Mother (primordial womb) herself as well as with various developmental theories. (Neumann saw Eros as perhaps mother's greatest gift to her infant.) The apples also raise the question of immortality—and so both green and yellow are represented in its red-hued symbolism—both Christian (Eve's forbidden fruit) and pre-Christian (the apples of Iduna or Hera). This, as we have seen, is a question preoccupying our comrades-in-arms.

Typical of fairy tales, it is only on the third try that the hero-prince finds out his true friend, a young man, also eighteen years old, also bound for the shrine of St. James. When the stranger takes the small piece of the apple, we are told that "the heart of the king's son was glad within him," and that he immediately proclaimed the youth his brother: "What is mine shall be thine, and what is thine shall be mine."[298] The stranger agrees to the proposition and, vowing to remain together no matter what might befall them, they set out as brothers—so similar in every respect, in fact, that we might even say, as twins. The entire scene recalls David and Jonathan's resolution of brotherhood in 1 Samuel.

---

[296] "How to Find Out a True Friend," *The Crimson Fairy Book,* p. 352.
[297] See above, p. 9.
[298] Ibid., p. 354.

The hero-prince and his true friend, having traveled for most of a year in quest of St. James's shrine, arrive one day at a city ruled by a scheming king. The king likes the looks of the prince, invites him to the palace and fêtes him, tolerating his friend until the opportunity arises to get rid of him. He is opposed not only to the friend, however, but also to the pilgrimage for which the friendship becomes a metaphor—or vice versa. The remainder of the tale is chiefly concerned with the attempts of the true friends to survive the divisive machinations of the king. In the end, it is once again the strength of erotic commitment that proves to be the most efficacious healing agent. This commitment demands a sacrifice from the prince similar to that demanded of Amile, his fore-runner: he must slay his child and smear his friend's body with the child's blood. Though repelled, he performs this macabre baptism, knowing that friendship—here truly sealed in blood—is more valuable than any new potential without that friendship. It is significant, I think, that the child is the scheming king's grandchild, and so symbolizes feminine potential on the side of the fathers as well as the prince's obligations to that father world, namely marriage and child-rearing.

I have spent time on this tale because although, as with Amis and Amile, green and yellow appear as an interchange of values between the two friends rather than strictly divided roles, it nevertheless makes quite clear the archetypal forces at work. Behind the green is Mother with her wise Eros. The prince's connection to the Queen Mother is kept alive throughout by his erotic commitment to his friend. This was, after all, the real fruit of her apple test. It is also to his mother's realm that he returns, having fulfilled his duty to the father world and having won for himself a wife, an erotic pledge, from that world. It is the queen who provides a home for him, his wife, his child and, later, his friend.[299] It is the queen, too, who seeks help for the friend when he lies dying. And, in this part, she takes on the characteristics of *mater dolorosa* together with mother of perpetual help, a role she was to play often in First World War imagery, as in Edmund Blunden's poem, "1916 Seen from 1921," where "Sweet Mary's shrine between the sycamores," bright as blood, offered "my friend of friends and [me]" refuge "from the grudging wars."[300] In short, mother's entirely green contribution to her son's growth is that of loving and nurturing life.

Behind the yellow is St. James. At the beginning of the tale, we are told that the queen's difficulties in conceiving a son—or were they her husband's difficulties?—demanded the intervention of a power outside her own sphere of influence. This came in the form of St. James. At the end, too, when the queen's efforts alone are not enough to revive the dying friend, St. James comes to the rescue.

---

[299] This ménage of husband, wife and male friend is like the conclusion of several fairy tales including Grimms' "The Frog King" and "The Golden Bird."

[300] Parsons, *Men Who March Away*, p. 176.

He is a spiritual representative of the best of the patriarchal tradition, a tradition exemplified in Christ's exhortation to his followers to leave mundane concerns and follow him or, in even more relevant words, "Greater love has no man than this, that a man lay down his life for his friends."[301] James represents the refining process, the supreme test of that Eros born in blood. But it is his efforts working in conjunction with those of the queen that produce the full miracle, the miracle of undying love, of which Christ is again the most differentiated exponent in our culture.

In modern Western civilization it is rather the mother's gifts that come as a shock when they show up in men and especially in male-male relationships. Their appearance has considerable dramatic impact, a circumstance that justifies their place in myths and stories where the setting—like a battlefield—is distinctly opposed to such gifts, to the Mother herself. Even when the contrast is not directly pointed out, it works its effect, as in the image of Achilles binding Patroclus's arm or Jonathan securing David's escape from Saul's wrath. In the many stories of Orestes' attempts to have the curse on the House of Atreus revoked, he finds in Pylades a partner ready to invoke the patriarchal gods to spur him on—

> What of the future? What of the Prophet God Apollo,
> the Delphic voice, the faith and oaths we swear?
> Make all mankind your enemy, not the gods;[302]

—and then to tend him with a passionate tenderness—

> . . . The second man
> Was wiping foam from his friend's lips, supporting him,
> Shielding him with the finely-woven cloak he wore,
> Watching against the hail of blows, and still intent
> On helping and comforting his friend;[303]

—or, from one of Euripides' last plays, *Orestes,* to vow again his succor:

> Orestes: . . . suppose the Furies drive me mad?
> Pylades: Then I'll look after you.
> Orestes: When my sickness comes, to touch me is revolting.
> Pylades: Not to me.
> Orestes: Take care you get no infection from me.
> Pylades: Think no more of it.[304]

---

301 John 15: 13.
302 Aeschylus, *The Oresteia,* p. 217.
303 *Iphigenia in Tauris,* in Euripides, *Three Plays,* p. 140.
304 *Orestes and Other Plays,* p. 328. This exchange between Orestes and Pylades finds an echo in a scene in Forster's *Maurice,* where the title character ministers to

Here Orestes is clearly the solar hero, golden boy, and Pylades the green-man gardener. In *Henry V* we do not know who is who but the affective force of the mother's gifts wins the day in this account of the battle for Agincourt:

> Suffolk first died, and York, all haggled over,
> Comes to him, where in gore he lay insteeped,
> And takes him by the beard, kisses the gashes
> That bloodily did yawn upon his face.
> He cries aloud, "Tarry, my cousin Suffolk!
> My soul shall thine keep company to heaven.
> Tarry, sweet soul, for mine, then fly abreast,
> As in this glorious and well-foughten field
> We kept together in our chivalry!"
> . . . .
> So did he turn, and over Suffolk's neck
> He threw his wounded arm, and kissed his lips,
> As so espoused to death, with blood he sealed
> A testament of noble-ending love.[305]

Byron's heroes, the fair-haired Calmar, son of the azure-eyed Mora, and Orla, "dark haired . . . destroyer of heroes," demonstrate a similar capacity for devotion that transcends death, their love immortalized by Celtic bards. Lying wounded, like York with Suffolk, over Orla's torn body, Calmar musters a final tribute:

> Never more shall Calmar chase the deer of Morven with Orla. . . . What were the chase to me alone? Who should share the spoils of battle with Calmar? Orla is at rest. Rough was thy soul, Orla! yet soft to me as the dew of morn. It glared on others in lightning: to me a silver beam of night. Bear my sword to blue-eyed Mora; let it hang in my empty hall. It is not pure from blood: but it could not save Orla. Lay me with my friend. Raise the song when I am dark![306]

By his fair hair and elegiac role, Calmar is unquestionably yellow—though he has, curiously enough, a positive mother behind him (rather like Achilles'

---

the ailing Clive:

> Maurice lifted him out of bed and put him on the night stool. When relief had come he lifted him back.
> "I can walk: you mustn't do this sort of thing."
> "You'd do it for me."
> He carried the stool down the passage and cleaned it. Now that Clive was undignified and weak, he loved him as never before.
> "You musn't," Clive repeated, when he came back. "It's too filthy."
> "Doesn't worry me," said Maurice. (*Maurice*, p. 97)

[305] William Shakespeare, *Henry V,* act 4, scene 6, lines 11-19, 24-27.
[306] *The Poetical Works of Lord Byron,* p. 41.

mother, Thetis)—and Orla, dark, rough, stormy, is green.[307] Finally, Walt Whitman, in "What Think You I Take my Pen in Hand?," shows us a male couple embracing amid the bustle of patriarchal industry.[308] We know nothing else of the participants, but what we see is clear enough: the compensating value of green as witnessed and recorded by a lunatic yellow man. Whitman made a kind of religion of the "dear love of comrades," as he called it, and, not inappropriately, chose for its emblem a plant, the calamus, a reed named after the Greek lover of Carpus.

Homoeros as a fitting way for men to reclaim for themselves some of the *terre fertile* of the mother's realm, so long disparaged and parceled out to women to tend—this, I think, is a major part of the message conveyed in the comrades-in-arms relationships we have so far looked at. Numerous twentieth-century examples of green and yellow comradeship employ the motifs of their less psychologically differentiated precursors: the battlefield setting; the emphasis on brotherhood and the equality of the partners; the tie of yellow to the patriarchal and green to the matriarchal; and the reevaluation, even reinstatement, of the latter as belonging to the masculine experience. To these we might add the conflict between undying love and physical death or between the mortal and immortal that such comradeships raise and seek to solve.

This last point dominates a novel by Yves Navarre, set in the first decades of this century, as much as it does Gilgamesh's mourning for Enkidu or York's for Suffolk or Calmar's for Orla or any of the war poets' for their fallen men of the land. Roland Raillac can look forward to his suicide as it will reunite him with his recently deceased lover and *raison d'être:* "It starts all over again. How sweet to die with you, Joseph, my fertile earth."[309] With these sentiments he closes

---

[307] This division into fair and dark belongs to the general symbolism of Romantic narrative which borrows in turn from Renaissance typology and continues active even today. For instance in Albicocco's film of *Le grand Meaulnes* (1970), or Ivory's of *Maurice* (1987), or Peter Weir's 1982 movie of the Great War, *Gallipoli,* the heroes-friends are explicitly dark and fair. The one is usually earthier, more sensual, more sensation-oriented. (Ivory's Clive, unlike Forster's, was dark, and so a bit off type, but in the second half of the film Scudder's dark complexion fits his role well.) The other is more idealistic, dreamy. In other words, dark and fair represent green and yellow respectively. In *Gallipoli* it is the dark-haired hero's harrowing cry, as he arrives too late with the reprieve that would prevent his fair friend from having to go into battle, that dominates the final moments of the film—the cry and an image of his friend frozen mid-stride in the Turkish sunlight by the cold bullet of the enemy soldier. Thus, it is the reverse of Byron's scene where the fair-haired man is given the final words. The green man has only a howl to express his anguish, the yellow man in Byron has a poem.

[308] *The Complete Poems,* p. 165.

[309] *Le petit galopin de nos corps,* p. 221.

his journal, document of a shared life, and hands on their love to posterity. Two kinds of posterity: the mystic union after death and the legend that lives on.[310]

Outside of the war poetry, most twentieth-century fiction, including those novels set around a war, takes the conflict of mortal versus immortal and reworks it so that it becomes the query, "To love or not to love?" Love, of course, signifies an acceptance of life in its manifold dimensions, a saying yes to the rainbow; not to love is a denial of life and a cowardly submission to the grey. With the advancing century, these two possibilities become more and more tightly allied to the matriarchy and patriarchy respectively. Gone are the redeeming features of the patriarchal system as exemplified by St. James in "How to Find Out a True Friend." He has become a purely saturnine, not to say satanic, force threatening the very existence of the planet.

In this scheme of things, comrade love between yellow and green champions a separation of the masculine from the patriarchal and, sometimes concomitantly but not always so, an overt alliance with the matriarchal. I have already shown evidence of similar tactics in stories as old as David and Jonathan's or the hero-friends of the Sicilian tale. However, in the twentieth century, these tactics take center stage.

As early as 1913, Forster's *Maurice* portrayed the struggle of a young, not very bright but solid pillar of the upper middle class attempting to extricate himself from the expectations his class and culture held for him. The first part of his struggle involves an emotional and spiritual awakening at the hands of a Cambridge scholar, Clive; he is permitted to love Clive passionately but platonically. Clive is the Hellenic yellow initiator, speaking to him of *Phaedrus* and *The Symposium,* and Maurice is the flower boy and intellectual bumpkin led irrevocably to a recognition of who and what he is—forced to accept the reality of his sexual identity in a world hostile to what the character of the Dean calls "the unspeakable vice of the Greeks."[311] Dumped by Clive, who finds he prefers power and position to the passionate attachment of his friend, Maurice defines a persona for himself, a blue-man position in the family strockbroking firm. Behind this he might have disappeared without trace if the ancient call for renewal had not arrived in the form of Clive's "inferior" (and shadow), the servant,

---

[310] Roland, though equipped with a green man's constitution, is otherwise the yellow man of the tale; he is the recorder after all. And his friend, Joseph, with his surname Terrefort and his strong mother ties, with his dreaminess, and his physical frailty, is a flower boy surely. Navarre's novel is, to my knowledge, one of the few outside a war setting to take a solution that, romantic as it may be in its excessiveness, is still anti-life. Suicide defies the archetypal pattern of green-yellow comradeship in which the green man's death is an inspiration to the yellow to go on living and creating.

[311] *Maurice,* p. 50.

undergamekeeper Alec Scudder (alias green man, gardener type).

Maurice finds that Alec, too, is a prisoner of the system and, in attempting to free Alec as well as himself, he graduates to the yellow role, true complement to Alec's green. We see this quite vividly demonstrated in the scene prior to Alec's proposed emigration to the New World when Maurice presents arguments for Alec's abandoning his plans. They are fantasies, yes, but also visions:

> "It's a chance in a thousand we've met, we'll never have the chance again and you know it. Stay with me. We love each other."
> "I dessay, but that's no excuse to act silly. Stay with you and how and where? What'd your Ma say if she saw me all rough and ugly the way I am?"
> "She never will see you. I shan't live at my home."
> "Where will you live?"
> "With you."
> "Oh, will you? No thank you. My people wouldn't take to you one bit and I don't blame them. And how'd you run your job, I'd like to know?"
> "I shall chuck it."
> "Your job in the city what gives you your money and position? You can't chuck a job."
> "You can when you mean to," said Maurice gently. "You can do anything once you know what it is." He gazed at the greyish light that was becoming yellowish. Nothing surprised him in this talk. What he could not conjecture was its outcome. "I shall get work with you," he brought out: the moment to announce this had now come.
> "What work?"
> "We'll find out."
> "Find out and starve out."
> "No. There'll be enough money to keep us while we have a look round. I'm not a fool, nor are you. We won't be starving. I've thought out that much, while I was awake in the night and you weren't."[312]

When his arguments fail to convince Alec (or so it seems), he is led to the crushing conclusion that, "Love was an emotion through which you occasionally enjoyed yourself. It could not do things."[313]

"Love as something that does things" is a nice definition of the kind of love existing in green-yellow comradeship. Among the things it often achieves is the consolidation of the individual as a counter-collective force for change in which the green provides the fertile ground for the sprouting of the yellow's visions. In *Maurice*, Alec finally does consent to play his part in the archetypal pattern, and, according to the original epilogue of the novel (unfortunately suppressed), Maurice and Alec take up the life of woodcutters. Like Thoreau in *Walden*, they create a new-old order in man's relationship with the natural world.

---

[312] Ibid., pp. 202-203.
[313] Ibid., p. 204.

Xavier Mayne's *Imre,* published six years before Forster penned *Maurice,* does not go to such lengths. The future of its protagonists, the athletic Hungarian soldier, Imre, and the fair-haired Northerner, Oswald, is unknown in its details. However, at the end of the novel they stand in Oswald's window, overlooking the city at night, an image of solidarity, an island of dawning consciousness emerging from a mass of evasions, disguises and conventions. Just as it is Alec's role to bring out the hero in Maurice and Maurice's to bring out the man in him,[314] so it is Imre, the green man, who leads Oswald to the park where the latter heroically reveals his Uranian nature. His revelations inspire Imre in turn to unburden himself, to become a man, not a cipher. Although not as explicitly sexual as either Imre or Maurice, François Seurel, the narrator of *Le grand Meaulnes,* plays the same role for the novel's eponymous adventurer, providing at the end even nursing duties to Meaulnes' abandoned wife and child, in return for Meaulnes' confidence and a share in his imagination. This exchange appears constantly in the fiction where green-yellow comradeship rules.

With Jennifer Johnston's *How Many Miles to Babylon?,* the heroic act demanded of the yellow seems to be the destruction of the green itself. Jerry, the ostler, and Alexander, the aristocrat, are thrown together in the trenches of the First World War as they were once before in the meadows and streams of their Irish countryside. When Jerry is condemned to be shot for attempted desertion, Alex takes the law into his own hands and blows out Jerry's brains so that the latter does not have to face an impersonal death. As he pulls the trigger, Jerry is singing an old Irish ballad about the stranger who comes seeking "Father Green." An expression of love, tenderness and sympathy becomes the heroic act in a setting where heroism has quite another meaning, colored by duty. The equation, love and tenderness = death, is a further indictment of the warmonger's world, here represented by the English captain who condemns Jerry to death. There is some triumph though, for Alex shows he has understood what is valuable to the green soul and is willing to sacrifice himself to provide that.

John and David's friendship, in Susan Hill's *Strange Meeting,* stands too as a solitary light amid the horrors of trench-life and the carnage of battle. Whereas the lesson in tenderness Alex masters with Jerry's help brings him before the firing squad as well—no one is permitted to interfere with army procedures—the lesson John learns from David against all the odds, both circumstantial and personal, does not die with David, with the man of the land's death; in a sense, his life blossoms, nurtured by his unshakeable love for David. The lesson is an appreciation for the joyful, loving, hopeful, curious, enthusiastic expressions of life. In the novel's last scene, John, now minus one leg (a typical yellow fate),

---

[314] Ibid., p. 208.

is conducted by a young farmer to David's family home. The home and John's journey represent a new epoch in the relationship of yellow to green:

> The car turned up the lane and then they were driving into the sun.
> "This is all my father's land, on either side of here. You can't see our farmhouse, it lies in the dip beyond the beeches there."
> The engine was grinding slowly up the hill. Then, they came out between the trees and saw the whole valley, sloping up gently to east and west. The sky was vast, darkening behind them.
> "There's the house."
> Hilliard looked up, and ahead.[315]

A shell-shocked victim from the battle of the Somme (1916), Francis Croft, poet, genius, yellow man, is unable to recover the tie to life which his green-man lover, Harvey, attempts to supply in Hill's *The Bird of Night*. He drifts further into madness and finally takes his life with a pair of garden shears—an image of madness as life turned against itself. Is this a legacy of his war experience? The book is unusual in that its narrator is the green man. It is a loving testimony of how green provides the ground and so the challenge to yellow. In this way it resembles *Le grand Meaulnes* where a green man is also narrator, and, as in *Meaulnes*, it is a challenge unheeded. Seize life, bring your visions into life, is what Harvey might have said to Francis. In late life, a feeble and lonely old man, Harvey is still able to devour life in true green fashion.

> Mrs Mumford brings me a jar of strawberry jam and I eat it, dipping in a spoon and taking great, dark goblets into my mouth, the taste is sweet and ripe. I am no longer so fastidious. On some nights I sleep here on the sofa in my clothes, wrapped in a rug, and the gentle, warm air of summer comes to me through the open window. I am as happy as when I slept under the hedges of Southern Italy as a very young man, and woke when there were still stars, fading before the seeping daylight. I remember the smell of the dry grass crushed beneath me, the taste of it against my mouth, I remember the figs bought at dawn from a farmer's wife and eaten, one after another until they were gone, I can feel my teeth biting into the fat, bland flesh. But all that was before I met Francis, when I still had my own future, like an undiscovered city at my feet.[316]

Then he adds, "It was insignificant. I would not wish for that time again."[317]

Now that he has lived with Francis and his soaring yellow spirit, the world of sensation is no longer sufficient unto itself. In just this point, we see the challenge of green-yellow comradeship from the green perspective: the possibilities lurking behind the appearance of things, to recognize the spirit in the matter.

---

[315] *Strange Meeting*, p. 179.
[316] *The Bird of Night*, pp. 50-51.
[317] Ibid., p. 51.

Mary Renault's *The Charioteer,* set during the Second World War, again focuses on the green man. His name is Laurie, his nickname "Spud" (potato), after his Irish ancestry. He is a mother's son. Father's departure from the scene takes place when Laurie is a mere child. As a young man, wounded at the battle of Dunkirk, he finds himself torn by his love for Ralph, a Hellenic naval hero, and Andrew, a conscientious objector and golden boy. On the surface, the novel is a simple love triangle, its challenges untypical of the comrades-in-arms genre. Below the surface, however, Laurie and Ralph both struggle to hold on to happiness and integrity, not only in opposition to a disapproving heterosexual world, but also to a precious homosexual scene that thrives on high drama and bitchiness. Ralph delivers an almost red-neck speech against this scene at one point, loaded with guilt and self-apology:

> "We all have to use the network sometime. Don't let it use you, that's all. Ours isn't a horizontal society, it's a vertical one. Plato, Michelangelo, Sappho, Marlowe; Shakespeare, Leonardo and Socrates if you count the bisexuals—we can all quote the upper crust. But at the bottom—Spud, believe me, there isn't any bottom. Never forget it. You've no conception, you haven't a clue, how far down it goes."[318]

Nevertheless, it is Ralph's unbending idealism, his insistence on clarity and light, that brings Laurie to recognize his own path. If Ralph challenges Laurie with the typical yellow-man idealism, Laurie's challenge to Ralph at the end of the novel is typically green, a challenge to live. Having been rejected by Laurie through a gross misunderstanding, Ralph contemplates suicide. Laurie discovers Ralph's plan by accident and, without letting Ralph know he knows, he offers himself as a kind of ground by which Ralph might reconnect to life:

> Remorse, even the greatest, has the nature of a debt; if we could only clear the books, we feel that we should be free. But a deep compassion has the nature of love, which keeps no balance sheet; we are no longer our own. So in the presence of this helpless forgiveness, Laurie seemed to himself to be doing only what was nearest in the absence of time to think. There was something here to be done which no one else could do. All the rest would have to be thought about later. He looked Ralph straight in the eyes, believing what he said.
> "... I should have come, anyway. I should have had to come back."[319]

The novel's last image, discussed in chapter two under the Hellenist, depicts another island of solidarity, very similar to *Imre's,* where green and yellow, the battle temporarily lulled, find some consolation in one another's embrace.

The finale of Ursula Zilinsky's *Middle Ground* (1968) is far more buoyant

---

[318] *The Charioteer,* p. 203.
[319] Ibid., p. 393.

than Renault's, though its main setting, a remote Nazi labor camp, is more harrowing. Her green-yellow protagonists are a twenty-year-old, spoiled, saucy, but likeable half-Jewish Prussian boy named Tyl von Pankow, and the disaffected, wasted camp commandant wounded in Africa fighting with Rommel's famous Korps, General von Svestrom.

Tyl's fatal beauty, his aristocratic ties, his louche shadow suggest the flower boy—von Svestrom offers him at one point a tribute of snowdrops—but principally he shows himself as a golden boy—high-flying, idealistic, given to fighting for causes rather than relationship, avoiding too close commitments. Von Svestrom's world-weariness, his self-loathing, his seeking solace in alcohol and Proust, have some of that self-destruction one finds in the lunatic type, but beneath is his profound belief that only love counts, only love can heal the division between Tyl and him. It is he who finds joy in the simple things of life—the snowdrops, for example; it is he who is proud owner of land by the sea. Beneath his broken exterior lurks a prophet of the land, infinitely wise, if occasionally despairing, in his quest for renewal through loving.

The two are thrown together in the camp during an outbreak of cholera. Tyl is quarantined in von Svestrom's quarters and they fall in love. It is not easy; Tyl will not let von Svestrom forget his position (disaffected though the latter is). They grapple, sometimes as older-younger, but always seeking to find some kind of equal footing, that is, true comradeship. It is Tyl who cannot accept it. They part. The war ends. Tyl disappears into the underworld of Vienna, von Svestrom into Allied military custody. And then they find one another again. For Tyl, golden boy, reunion means verification of von Svestrom's statement that the real enemies are the people who draw lines. Verification is armistice and the end of his initiation. They can be comrades now.[320]

There are many more fictional examples of green-yellow comradeship demonstrating similar concerns, but here I think we must stop and ask how this picture tallies with a much-quoted statement by that architect of Jungian thought, Erich Neumann.

In his monumental study of consciousness, Neumann places Eros between men in the realm of self-defense against the Terrible Mother:

> Accentuation of the man-to-man relationship eventually leads to the overthrow of the matriarchate by patriarchal rulers. Just as in Sparta, with its late matriarchal conditions, a strongly marked masculine relationship is to be observed among pairs of young warriors, so, at a much earlier date, we

---

[320] We might well ask why so many chroniclers of green-yellow comradeship have been women. Besides Susan Hill, Jennifer Johnston, Mary Renault and Ursula Zilinsky mentioned in this book, there are many others, all showing a remarkable sensitivity to the green-yellow dynamic between men.

find the same thing in the Gilgamesh Epic and numerous other hero myths. The countless male friendships in Greek mythology vindicate themselves, like that between Gilgamesh and Engidu, in the hero's fight with the Great Mother dragon.[321]

The key word here is "vindicate." Without the necessity of slaying the mother-fiend, such friendships could apparently not be vindicated. Some years later, in *The Child,* Neumann took up this theme again. Outlining in a truly bravura fashion the successive stages of ego development in the infant, he compared them to the evolution of consciousness in the so-called primitive man.[322] Noteworthy stages common to both the infantile ego and primitive man's separation from the mother/Mother are the "magic-phallic" and "magic-warlike" stages. Here Neumann places the phenomenon of male-male bonding among "primitives" and in so doing proclaims its immature nature. But, is he just in his assessment?

One can certainly view the attachments of Gilgamesh and Enkidu or Orestes and Pylades as involving, at least as part of their purpose, a defeat of the Terrible Mother. However, this does not in any way define the main value or thrust of these relationships. And, what about David and Jonathan? Achilles and Patroclus? Calmar and Orla? Maurice and Alec? Or most of the other comrades in-arms we looked at? With them the enemy is very clearly masculine and, what's more, patriarchal. It would be begging the issue, as Neumann seems to do, that the source of such struggles as these pairs endure is nothing more than mother-in-disguise. In *God and the Gods,* Walter Beltz writes,

> Patriarchy is the primeval form of alienation, and so there appear along with it class distinctions, private property, exploitation and the state.[323]

We might also add the concept of duty—to state, church, social conventions, etc.—which is often experienced as alienating to one's own nature as well as to Nature herself. So, at least, we heard Jonathan intimating in Charpentier's opera, *David et Jonathan.* Orestes is also tormented by his duty to the father world (prescribed in Apollo's decree) as are Navarre's Roland and Joseph, Forster's Maurice and Alec, Zilinsky's Tyl and Johannes. And in the Sicilian tale, the prince's duties as husband and father weigh in against the deeper commitment to his friend. Or, psychologically speaking, to wholeness or Self. Later, writing about the Yahwist source of Old Testament texts, Beltz amplifies this theme:

> Yahweh is the god of . . . war. He looks after the aims of the patriarchy, where males have seized and hold power. The matriarchal "Golden Age" was

---

[321] *The Origins and History of Consciousness,* pp. 180-181.
[322] *The Child,* pp. 136-179.
[323] *God and the Gods: Myths of the Bible,* p. 22.

over. . . . Now wars were waged, lands conquered, foreigners exploited, centralized political authority established. All this required laws and regulations, and Yahweh enacted them. In order to maintain such laws and guarantee their observance, judges and soldiers were brought in. Private property, family law, exploitation and statist ideology all underwent a broad development. . . . It was an act of virtue to wage war. The monarchy was a god-given institution and obedience to the royal priests was commanded by law. Women were looked upon as less valuable, important only as the mothers of children.[324]

This image of the emerging patriarchy in the ancient Holy Land, particularly its emphasis on war, is echoed in Kenneth Dover's study of Greek homosexuality, in which he speaks of the political fragmentation of the Greek world:

The Greek city-state was continuously confronted with the problem of survival in competition with aggressive neighbours, and for this reason the fighter, the adult male citizen, was the person who mattered.[325]

This then is the world where legends of great male friendships were formed and widely circulated. It is not a world lacking in the kind of solar consciousness Neumann claims such friendships served to secure. Rather than seeing them as lending support to a patriarchal culture struggling to consolidate itself out of its matriarchal sources, we should perhaps see this manifestation of Eros as playing a mediating role between matriarchal and patriarchal forces, as, once again, a healer. It is homoeros that draws men together in defiance of alienation, as Beltz would have it, and death; in short, a compensation for a mandate that proclaims, "Destroy!"

I wrote earlier that the initiatory homosexuality of the Greeks, Albanians, Melanesians, etc., provided an outlet for the warrior to express his love toward his own sex and that without this outlet severe psychic disturbance, on both personal and collective levels, might occur. This is just as true of the comrades-in-arms relationship where struggle, if not always war, is the typical framework. However, except in extraordinary situations like the Theban band, homoeros is viewed by the patriarchy as inimical to its aims (compare Beltz) because it moves to right the imbalance which patriarchy imposes by means of alienation.

The enmity between homoerotic phenomenon and patriarchal values remains topical. Very recently we have had vivid representations of it in commercial films like *The Kiss of the Spider Woman, The Fruit Machine* and *My Beautiful Laundrette,* the last of which shows how the extreme conditions of Thatcher's Britain (a patriarchal kingdom if ever there was one) provoked a homosexual

---

[324] Ibid., p. 23.
[325] *Greek Homosexuality,* p. 201.

resistance. In the same vein, British singer-songwriter Mark Knopfler sings in
"Brothers in Arms":

> These mist covered mountains
> Are home now for me
> But my home is the lowlands
> And it always will be
> Someday you'll return to your valleys and your farms
> And no longer burn to be brothers in arms.

> Through these fields of destruction
> Baptisms of fire
> I have witnessed your suffering
> As the battle raged higher
> And though it had hurt me so bad then
> In the fear and alarm
> You did not desert me, my brothers in arms.[326]

Taking these visions one step farther, the young hero of David Rees's novel
In the Tent (1979) fantasizes a war-torn country healed through the creative co-
operation of homosexual pairs like himself and "John." The setting of the fantasy is Britain after the civil war in 1649:

> The young man . . . turned round and stared.
> "Stranger?" he asked.
> "Yes."
> "Looking for work?"
> "Yes."
> "There is plenty to be done. . . . Fields overgrown with weeds, animals
> to be fed, thatch to repair, cooking and cleaning. You can help me if you
> wish."
> "I would like to."
> . . . .
> "I'll show you the farm . . . Can you thatch a roof?"
> "I can learn."
> "Good."
> "I'll start in here." Tim surveyed the kitchen: piles of unwashed dishes,
> half-eaten food, a blocked sink, a smoking fire. "I can cook."
> "I have little or no money, but we can share everything, if that suits
> you."
> "It will."[327]

Here, in Tim's fantasy, the meeting of comrades-in-arms, green (John) and
yellow (Tim), is very explicitly an antidote to patriarchal power struggles.

Beneath this attempt to mediate or reconcile the imbalance stands, as I indi-

---

[326] Dire Straits recording, Polygram, 1985.
[327] *In the Tent*, pp. 120-122.

cated, an alliance to the principles of the Great Mother. This of all its faults, perhaps, makes homoeros threatening to the patriarchy. It is chiefly for this reason that homoeros has been so severely chastened in our Judeo-Christian civilization—by, among others, Jung and Neumann. Mother is dangerous—even, it seems, her positive, life-giving, life-sustaining, life-celebrating aspects —and must be slain at all costs. These are after all what is expressed by the erotic merger of green and yellow comrades-in-arms. In our examples, it is this Eros, rather than the Great Mother herself, that takes a front-line position—the green always a little ahead of the yellow—in the fight against a venal and grudging patriarchal tradition which alienates, promising only godless death as its fruit.

One might argue that the tradition is valuable at least for providing a proving ground for the honing of male and male-male Eros, and so it is—to a point. Alienation is as much an archetypal force as its opposite and belongs to the drama of life; perhaps without war and ecological disaster men would never recognize the importance of seeking the healing Eros in and among themselves, or see that Eros as well as aggression is an issue between men. But it is a big price to pay for awareness. In this twilight of the patriarchal gods, we might also argue that we cannot really afford another war, another dead sea, another poisoned landscape. Men must find another way to love each other.

Achilles binding Patroclus, detail of a bowl of Sosias, ca. 500 B.C.
(Antiquarium, Berlin)

4
Case Material

Now that I have sketched the principal components of the green-yellow dialogue, let us see what it looks like in the lives of modern men. I will present the case of Hannes, a thirty-five-year-old North German stage director who was studying European art history at the University of Zürich. This will be supplemented with extracts from five other cases, three featuring exclusively homosexual men, the other two demonstrating some homosexual experience within a predominantly heterosexual orientation. With these we will find both varieties of green-yellow relationship, deploying the full gamut of motifs common to such relationships, especially those of light and nature.

Hannes and Nino—Preliminary Remarks

Hannes is a tall, fair-haired man with an expressive face and voice. The latter he clearly used to his advantage in his successful career as director for experimental theater in the large industrial city that was also his hometown. Many of his projects involved mixed media—the spoken word, music, mime, circus, dance—and it was during his work on one of these that he met Nino, a modern dancer of Austro-Italian parentage. This was eleven years before I met him.

Nino was twenty, four years younger than Hannes. Their relationship lasted seven years; for a large part of this time, they lived together. It came to an end when Nino fell in love with another dancer and moved away. Two years after the break-up, unable to continue his work in the theater with any enthusiasm, plagued with a gastro-intestinal disorder and, in a word, depressed, Hannes responded to a friend's invitation to make a break in Zürich and enrolled in the university there. Shortly after, he entered analysis.

Hannes had been in therapy once before, in an attempt to understand the possessiveness he often experienced in regard to Nino—it was a source of some conflict in their relationship—but, as the therapist was basically unsympathetic to homosexuality, little light was shed on the problem. When Hannes first came to see me, he was extremely anxious about his move to Zürich, his new studies, the lack of familiar surroundings. He had found cheap accommodation in a modernish apartment block, which he described as aesthetically hideous. It also had very thin walls through which he could hear his neighbors' every move and this gave him the feeling of having no privacy, of never being "at home." Such conditions exacerbated his anxiety, which at times would be so pronounced as to resemble panic attacks, complete with fear, disorientation, palpitations, hyperventilation, sweating and an aggravation of his bowel problems. He hated, he said, changing environments. He had always reacted to physical changes the same way, except, he maintained, when he and Nino were together. Nino had no fear of the physical world. Right after making this distinction between Nino and himself, Hannes had the following dream:

> Nino and I are reunited in the bedroom of my parents' old home. We make love. Before we finish, Frau Müller, the neighbor lady, comes to the door. I tell Nino to make himself scarce, but he doesn't. He comes out of the bedroom, naked, smiling, talks with Frau Müller in a friendly fashion; and she with him. I am surprised. Then, on the way back into the city, Nino tells me he has just taken a personality test and that he has turned out to be green, or, in the test's language, "A Frog." I smile and say that of course he's a frog, I've known it all along.

Hannes's associations to green were "growing," "alive," "natural." I asked him how he himself might come out on such a test and he answered immediately, "a yellow bird." We were on our way.

Anamnesis

When Hannes was born, his parents were already forty. He was their first child in fourteen years of marriage and he duly became the apple of his father's eye. Two years after his birth, a sister was adopted, but Hannes suffered no loss in status as a result. His father came from a dour, strict Lutheran family—one of his brothers was a pastor—professing a deep respect for propriety, law and order, reputation, success in the world. Hannes said that besides such values, his father had considerable musical and literary talent, but refused to honor them in any but a dilettantish, hit-and-miss way. When Hannes was a child, however, he felt his father encouraged his own creativity, especially his interest in the theater, by making him such things as puppets and a puppet theater and by taking him to see plays and operettas. In fact, says Hannes, his father was never more alive than in those years before Hannes reached puberty when he was showing his son the wonders of the theatrical world. When Hannes began to want to do and see things on his own, his father turned him into an enemy, a traitor. He could not brook his son's growing independence and regularly tried to embarrass or diminish his son with his superior knowledge and "common sense."

At about this time, Hannes showed the first symptoms of a rare neurological disease involving atrophy of the peripheral nerves and the muscles they feed. His father's reaction was to start drinking. Hannes was hurt by this; what he found especially hard to take was his father's attempts to hide his drinking behind the perennially proper and responsible persona. His concern for the appearance of his home and family, for his performance in the world (he bought and sold property for the municipal government) increased. He became, like the father of John

Hilliard in *Strange Meeting* or Alex Moore in *How Many Miles to Babylon?*, obsessive about details like gardens, eaves, automobiles. Like them, too, he was a broken or "hollow" man (as T.S. Eliot named the type), harboring a deep sense of failure, which he tried to dispel with alcohol. The diagnosis of Hannes's illness when he was seventeen only heightened his father's feelings of failure; it was, after all, a blot on the family appearance. He retreated more and more into a world of morose thoughts. When Hannes left home at the age of nineteen to live with friends, his father was deep into the study of Dracula and vampirism.

The portrait I have drawn of Hannes's father gives, I hope, a sense of the great impact and influence the father's world had—typically—on the development of this yellow man. It was without doubt the predominating influence. It mixed a strict adherence to Lutheran values and social conformity with a spirit that longed, but was not permitted, to soar. On the one hand, Hannes's illness somatized his father's problem; on the other, Hannes, through his developing interest in the theater, did his father's soaring for him. His father clearly had a heavy narcissistic investment in Hannes's life, which may explain the destructive reactions to his son's demands for independence as well as to the boy's illness.

Important as his father's influence was on his life, Hannes told me his first therapist had been largely dismissive of it and concentrated on his mother. Homosexuality always meant a mother problem to this therapist and, accordingly, Hannes's issues were always referred back to her. Hannes called it his therapist's fiction. I would say that though it pales next to the father problem, a mother problem is nonetheless present; indeed, the mother is integral to the structure of most father problems. Had Hannes's mother been different, the impact his father had on his life would also have been different.

Like Constance Hilliard in *Strange Meeting,* Hannes's mother was in love with her youth. She was in love with her large family and the peacefulness and harmony of life in the countryside where she was raised till the age of twelve. The city was not entirely foreign to his mother's family, as one of her ancestors had built the Liebfrauen Kirche there four hundred and fifty years earlier. Although she gave an impression of practicality, even earthiness, which met her husband's demands for a well-run household, Hannes's experience of her was of a mother absent, "lost to the past." She fed and clothed him, looked after him when he was sick or in trouble, but otherwise gave him no emotional support. She always deferred to her husband's feelings, which were anyway not to be resisted with impunity, and left her son and daughter—especially Hannes—in his emotional care. She sought refuge from her husband's authoritarian moods in religious tracts and long visits to her sisters living in Austria.

Several generations back, the family had been Catholic but following intermarriage with Protestants, Catholic practice had virtually disappeared from her family. The religious tracts she devoured were mostly those of a German guru of positive thinking. It was to this man that Hannes's mother turned in her meditative time, and as Hannes grew older his mother often quoted to him from the guru's wise sayings in hopes that Hannes, too, would become a disciple. In fact, it seems that his mother felt extremely lonely, isolated and impotent in her relationships with her husband and children and wanted Hannes as an ally, a companion; but she could not speak her feelings directly.

The mother's reticence, combined with the demands and expectations of the father—often expressed by moods, one such leading to the father's silence for three months when Hannes was seventeen—left Hannes rather insecure in the feeling realm. He rarely had appropriate emotional feedback from his parents. In his early relationships he often had the idea that his feelings were not good enough. He felt awkward and shy and covered it over with a theatricalism picked up from his contact with the world of play-making. Throughout his adolescence, the theater had been a definite escape route from the emotional confusion at home and particularly from his father's drinking problem. Hannes could not forgive the downfall of this self-styled oracle/god/magician of his childhood and so, when not hunting for his father's hidden bottles (always in the hope of finding none), he chose to live in an imaginary world where he could control the outcome of events.

I found similar backgrounds in two other analysands who were predominantly yellow and heterosexual. For Lukas, a twenty-eight-year-old diploma candidate in architecture, father also ruled the house with his moods while mother played the long-suffering martyr to her domestic role. She, too, hid behind the teachings of a German guru. There she could keep alive memories of a happy childhood in the Tyrolean Alps at the knee of a stern but loving father who was a Nazi doctor. The moods of Lukas's father were less manipulative than those of Hannes's—in fact, they would often erupt into violence and Lukas would be beaten—otherwise their range was similar. As with Hannes's father, Lukas's father's moods became progressively more extreme as he aged, finding an outlet in sentimentality and morbidity.

In the case of Darius, twenty-five-year-old jazz musician and golden boy par excellence—well over six feet tall, with shining blond hair and a champion swimmer's physique, he could easily be called an Apollo—the father has stuck with unswerving faithfulness to the British public-school values in which he was reared. So locked in is he by this value system of fair play, law and order, and propriety, that he has become a bit unreal, says Darius, unreal and inaccessible. Darius has inherited the weight of that value system. (He once dreamt of his father lying heavily on his back.) It is a burden that no doubt accounts in part for Darius's chronic back problem as well as much of the "good-boy" behavior that colors and falsifies his own relationships. It was probably such unrealness in her husband's feelings for her that prompted Darius's mother seven years ago to demand a divorce—"out of the blue," Darius says. She has more of the black rage and power of Alex's mother in *How Many Miles to Babylon?*[328] than either Lukas's or Hannes's mother; she is something of a Clytemnestra, her sudden demand for divorce like the fatal blow Clytemnestra dealt Agamemnon. Darius's mother, however, was like the other two in her worship of her father.

It would seem that each of these women accepted a husband who would in no way challenge or interfere with their memories of father, and that these golden memories were transferred somewhat narcissistically onto their sons who thus became for them not only their fathers but also their hope of salvation. Whether this is true or not to the same degree with each of our yellow men, they all played the role of mediator, peace-maker and preserver of the family fictions and fantasies; for these tasks intuition became their most reliable tool.

If we look for confirmation of Hannes's early experience at a predominantly homosexual yellow man, the pattern does not alter much. Corneliu, twenty-six-year-old painter-son of Romanian Jewish parents, grew up with a mother who, though noisier and more colorful than either Lukas's or Hannes's, was nonetheless a servant of her husband, insofar as her husband's hardline Communist views (Stalinist, in fact) set the ideological tone of the household. As a child, Corneliu won races and other athletic competitions and his medals were appropriated by father as evidence of the superiority of Communist child-rearing. In a similar way, Hannes's father had robbed him of his interest in the theater by using it as a mirror for his own pleasure. But where Hannes's interest survived the violation, Corneliu's did not. Today, he spurns competitive sport of any kind. With narcissistic ambitions coming at him from both sides, the yellow man's constitutional tendency to fly heavenward is naturally aggravated; but his solution, however, only plays into his parents' hands or visions—a divine child is what they most desire after all.

Corneliu, Darius and Hannes were helped, perhaps even saved, from irrevocable flight by the presence of a sister who refused on some level the golden ambitions of the family and was, in Darius's case anyway, directly critical of them. Hannes's adopted sister Sylvie was an outsider whose very different tempo and outlook constantly challenged the family to return to ground and confront the real world without their usual fantastic filters. Sensual, hedonistic, even amoral, Sylvie was constantly in trouble with the authorities, whether at home, at school or later in the office. She cheated, lied, stole, became pregnant in her teens; she drove her parents, especially her father who was so keen on shining

---

[328] Johnston, *How Many Miles to Babylon?*, p. 35.

Initiating spirit as dragon
(from Vitruvius, *De architectura, 1511*)

appearances, to distraction and made the well-behaved Hannes extremely nervous, even frightened. When speaking of her now, however, he can admit that she possessed a kind of Rabelaisian roguerie that made her a friend to Life. Viewed in this light, it was not surprising to him that Nino and Sylvie had been fond of one another.

When Hannes met Nino, he had had sexual experience only with older men. These were men working in the theater, principally yellow men who permitted Hannes to play the green youth or flower boy for a while. Like Hannes's father though, these men were impressed by his abilities and used them to a certain extent. Hannes flattered their notions of themselves as mentors. The sexual relations were stormy and mutually recriminatory for, as Hannes now says, he really did not want another father, he was already too yellow to play a convincing green youth. Nevertheless, he learned a lot from them; his work, in fact, still bears the positive imprint of those relationships and, interestingly, he occasionally still fantasizes about having sex (usually passive) with such figures.

This leads one to wonder again about the proximity of the two kinds of green-yellow relationship, their probable interdependence. Even with the heterosexual Lukas and Darius, these two relationships are discernible. One of Lukas's few homosexual encounters was with an older man, a wandering sage with a huge phallus who played the penetrating role. In dreams, Lukas finds himself most often erotically linked with age-mates, young men with a so-called feminine side. For Darius, real-life homosexual experience has been confined to age-mates; in dreams he has experiences similar to Lukas's, with feminine men, but also, more vividly, with the kind of initiatory sexuality with an older man described in chapter three as man-youth relationships. The latter type allows for an experience of the power of the phallic masculine as something bigger than oneself, something that can possess one and to which one must humbly submit. "Being fucked," Hannes said, "was like having your head knocked off."

At the same time, as this implies, the initiatory relationship gives the younger, passive partner an experience of his receptivity, his ground and groundedness, his greenness in fact. The other type, the comrades-in-arms relationship, permits an equal exchange of strikingly different values within a framework of solidarity that is mutually enriching for the partners and often even productive of a third possibility. We have already seen these points illustrated in previous sections and we will see them again in the life and dream examples that follow.

With Nino, Hannes discovered his own yellow power as both mentor and comrade. Nino, it seems, made a similar discovery from his green position. In Hannes's most lunatic periods, when Hannes was really "flying," Nino even played mentor in the style of a Boyard or Zorba, reminding Hannes of the beauty and wisdom of "ground," so that he didn't lose himself. (Of course, all my in-

formation about Nino comes through Hannes, so it is colored by his perceptions, complexes, etc., but it is perfectly believable when seen beside the other
examples I have offered. Even if it were all fantasy and fabrication, it would be a
valuable addition to our tapestry for it reflects the same archetypal dynamics.)

Nino, as I have said, came from a mixed Austro-Italian family. His mother
was what Hannes called a typical Italian mother, emotional, intense, at times to
the point of being hysterical, and devoted to the welfare of her three children. She
was a painter, a water-colorist, of whose work the whole family was proud. Her
husband was rather quieter, less present on the whole than his wife (partly as a
result of the traveling demanded by his work). When he was home, he tended to
be an observer, a foil for his wife's energy. Hannes told me that Nino's father
also sometimes drank too much, but without the secrecy of his own father; he
drank to relax after a hard week rather than to forget. Nino and his sisters resem-
bled him more than they did their mother. Temperamentally, they tended to be
quiet, calm, even somewhat passive.

Nino enjoyed good food and drink. He loved to cook and would often prepare
special meals for Hannes and himself. Home, he often told Hannes, was the
most important thing to him. While they lived together, Nino spent hours
searching for inspiration in Italian interior design magazines; their combined
salaries never permitted more than a fraction of this inspiration to find concrete
means of expression, but still Nino drew plans. Outside their apartment, on their
terrace, Nino applied his nesting energies to growing vegetables and flowers.

In all of these activities, Nino reminds me of two other analysands, twenty-
four-year-old Thierry, a French student, and forty-two-year-old Willi, a book illustrator. Green men both, they, too, have pronounced domestic instincts. Willi,
Hannes's Zürich-based friend who offered him refuge there, insists on working
out of his home where he can keep an eye on his vast garden, and Thierry expressed his desire to work as a translator out of a country home surrounded by
animals and plants.

Nino was a good dancer, according to Hannes. With a solid technique, he cut a
very sturdy, masculine figure on stage. It was Nino-as-dancer that first attracted
Hannes and, perhaps because his own physical handicap demanded a dancer-lover,
he failed to appreciate fully Nino's preference for home over career. Hannes
pushed Nino in his career and through his influence and encouragement Nino
made considerable progress. It was here, in his fostering of his friend's career,
that Hannes demonstrated his ability to play the yellow mentor role. This, in
turn, gave him a sense of confidence in himself. Nino, for his part, provided
Hannes with a kind of forum, a physical home to be sure, but more, too, where
Hannes would feel free to express feelings too long bottled up. Nino listened and
by listening brought Hannes to hear his own words, to feel his own ideas, gauge

his own intensity. This, as I said above, was a grounding, centering experience for him. Nino, of course, looked after those details of daily routine that Hannes's handicap made difficult for him, but what was most important, Hannes now says, was Nino's calm, reliable nourishment of Hannes's Muse. Hannes made many of his most important theatrical works during this period, and in most of them Nino found a place to show what he could do as a performer.

At the time neither realized the potential of such a relationship, according to Hannes, and falling prey to the neurotic excesses of their types—gardener and lunatic—they failed to set appropriate limits or differentiate existing boundaries. Nino thought he wanted more freedom, Hannes less. The reverse was actually true, Hannes now says. Hannes became jealous and possessive, Nino correspondingly freer in his sexual relations with others. Both felt betrayed, abandoned.

Nino went on tour with a dance company (which Hannes's influence had arranged) and fell in love with a dancer who was not as demanding or "complicated" as Hannes. Hannes says that at first he was relieved when Nino left, but later became desperate. He fell ill with a mild gastro-intestinal disorder that eventually turned into a chronic bowel problem. Only shortly before his move to Zürich was it treated effectively. He sees the whole period now as typical of the yellow man's insecurity in the mother realm, typical of the fragility of his "home," in terms of physical space and emotional structure as well as of an inner center, which the bowels/belly also symbolize. His initial reaction to Nino's departure—relief—was a denial that the green foundation that had become so vital to his creativity had also disappeared; and without that, he risked disappearing into thin air.

Occasionally during our work together, Hannes complained that Nino's ways were always so foreign, so "other," and because of this were annoyingly inaccessible—that wasn't his world! And to a point certainly he was right, but he also admitted that when Nino left he lost contact with an often elusive, numinous part of himself. Nino had been the willing partner of this part of him for a time and Hannes, if he wanted to find it again, would have to go into himself. The move to Zürich and the resulting panic around the issue of home were the final straw. Hannes entered analysis.

The Course of the Analysis

Within two weeks of starting work, Hannes had the dream of Nino as frog/green-man cited above. Such green qualities as lack of embarrassment about the body and a good, easy relationship to the positive mother are clearly evident in Nino's dealings with Frau Müller. Hannes described her as a second mother, a generous-hearted woman who always gave him special treats as a child—he remembers especially glazed mandarin orange slices. He confirmed that Nino also possessed such features and that he often wished he could imitate him. His physical handicap, he said, always stood in the way; he could never manage it.

The next dream image of Nino, a couple of weeks later, again identified him with green and, what is more, contrasted that green sharply with yellow. It was following this dream that we began using the terms green and yellow to identify certain qualities and types of behavior. In this second dream, Hannes bid farewell to his two favorite teachers from primary school and the *Gymnasium* (high school), both positive mother figures who had unselfishly fostered his interest in the theater. He then found himself at the opera,

> a kind of celebration of my departure. The opera's leading character is Oberon, king of the fairies in Shakespeare's *A Midsummer Night's Dream*. I talk with him in a sparkling, dark green woods. Afterward, I embrace Nino. The embrace is very intense as we have both come to realize that there is an indissoluble bond between us, that it has never been broken.

Following this reconciliation, Hannes dreamt he was outside a lecture hall at his former university, where he had also come to bid adieu. He watched several people coming out of a workshop. He heard from one of them, an elegant woman friend, that the leadership of the workshop had been disappointing. Then the leader appeared, a former university acquaintance heavily involved in drugs. He was "spaced out, like some kind of Indian guru, wearing yellow: yellow shirt, yellow trousers." At this point, the woman tried to reassure him and he told her he was leaving.

This dream with its emphasis on saying good-by to old ways of learning makes very clear the timeless and ineradicable essence of the green-yellow mating. For Hannes, it showed that his link with the green, which had been forged via Nino, had to be recognized and sealed with a kiss. He had been changed, his soul touched by the green and he could not go back. By means of this change, he could now see, only too clearly, the dangers of a yellow way that was too one-sided. With this dream, Hannes really felt the need to stop looking for self-justifications and get down to an exploration of the meaning of his life with Nino. He also ceased his campaign of bitter resentment against Nino's memory. His panic, still lingering in the background, vanished and he was even offered a new and quiet home in a picturesque seventeenth-century house.

Two weeks later, Hannes had another dream of Nino in which his role in relation to the green man was clarified:

> An old city, surrounded by a plain. A young man, very simple, resembling Nino, wants to quit his job in the theater to study roses. I try to find a book for him which will be a history and aesthetic appreciation of roses. I know that I must look for something very simple, almost child-like, because he is not very comfortable with words. I find one that has many brightly-coloured

images of roses in it. He looks at the book with great pleasure, particularly one page showing four brilliant roses: yellow, red, orange and pink.

This simple Nino is the green youth for whom Hannes was yellow mentor, but he is also that simple, uneducated green aspect of Hannes himself that requires an erotic encounter with the ego Hannes in order to flower. Roses and other flowers, but especially roses, were from this point on to become a very common motif in his dreams. A year after his break-up with Nino, Hannes had converted to—rather rediscovered—Catholicism, and his dream roses often had a Catholic feel; sometimes they were directly linked to the Passion of Christ and the mission of Mary. At other times, as we shall see, they had a more secular or profane passion, but in either case they were speaking of a life lived not in the ether of yellow imagination, but in Eros, in relationship. Accepting the suffering such a life brings as well as its pleasures and deep, resonant joys, was at least part of the task Hannes had set himself in tracking down his own green.

Nino continued to play an important role in Hannes's unconscious life, but with the dream of the roses, other unknown carriers of green began to appear. One such figure borrowed roses to increase his impact:

> On a lush green bank in the sunlight, I sit facing a naked young man with shiny and perhaps slightly wet jet black hair. He is very—beautiful is the only word, like a god. Watching me as though trying to read my reactions to his "entertainment," he takes a rose petal and puts it in his hair above his ear. I find the gesture overwhelmingly sensual. He rubs rose petals into his crotch and then lets them fall over his shoulder and down his back with something like a moan or a cry of delight. He laughs and his laugh is like a bell. Then, he is clothed: a flame-colored velvet shirt and a pair of grey and white striped trousers. We are going to the theater.

"Like a god" is a telling phrase, for Hyacinthus, Cyparissus, Carpus and all the other beautiful flower boys beloved of gods and men in Greco-Roman mythology are, of course, gods themselves. A dream following shortly after this one even defined his field of divinity:

> I see a young man in a woodland scene, decked out in roses and leaves. I know he is a nature god. G. [the analyst] points to this image emphatically as if to say, "Yes, him!" After he does this, the smiling face of another young man appears over the nature god's chest.

Somewhat closer to Hannes was a dark-haired Englishman, his colleague in a language school (no such person or school existed in reality).

> He is swimming in a lily pond. He wears a black and white bathing suit (like those of the 1920s). After, while sunning himself on a Monet-like bridge, he pulls the straps from his shoulders and exposes his back and chest. I compliment him on his appearance in a flowery way. He glows under my "Italian" admiration. I know he is willing to be seduced.

To England and Englishmen, Hannes immediately associated Forster's *Maurice*, the film of which he had just seen. He also noted the similarity between this man's coloring, his black-and-white bathing suit and his seductiveness, and the rose-petal youth of the earlier dream.

In all these dreams, the physical beauty of Hannes's male partner is stressed. Hannes confessed his attraction to beautiful young men—especially to dancers, as we've seen—and he himself pointed up the obvious compensatory nature of such attraction. Because none of these men corresponded to real men, I brought up the question of the dream's subjective message—what these men implied about Hannes himself—but Hannes could not hear it, as he could in no way conceive of himself as physically attractive. This made it very difficult for him to approach the type of young man he liked; he described himself on these occasions as painfully shy.

When he was with Nino, who appeared to appreciate him physically, Hannes's shyness sometimes led him into fits of self-loathing. He would lash out at the superficiality of beautiful men and their obsessive, even narcissistic concern with their own bodies. These attacks were doubly wounding: Nino felt them like a physical assault and closed himself off for extended periods—Hannes compared these to his father's silences—and Hannes's own self-respect reeled under the lashings so that later he felt ashamed. The relationship, too, suffered—both from Hannes's verbal brutality and from Nino's mute, uncomprehending retreats—but the archetypal power governing it always reasserted its authority and the lovers found themselves together again. This pattern persisted until one day Nino's retreat took him too far and the tension that had kept them bound (even at a distance) snapped like a string pulled too tightly, leaving Nino in another world.

We discussed many times ways in which Hannes might become more familiar with his body—exercising, swimming, massage, cooking, etc.—for clearly a large part of Nino's appeal for Hannes was the dancer's ability to communicate physically. Hannes was excited by the notion, but for a long time it remained just a notion. It was only in the last few months of our work together, when his illness seemed to advance slightly, that he understood "from the heart" what was necessary and began to look after himself.

Nonetheless, I felt that with the image of the handsome Englishman in the lily pond, appreciation of his own physical nature was coming closer to consciousness. A later dream image demonstrates further progress in this regard. In it, Hannes converses with a dark, solidly built but not at all beautiful university colleague—another mature student—named Enrico:

> He wears glasses and a green sweatshirt. We skirt around the issue of homosexuality. Is he—or not? Later, I receive from him a letter telling me of his

intention to perform a nude dance in Salzburg. I take this as a confession of his homosexuality. I prepare to answer him in kind.

Here homosexuality becomes a symbol of an integrity (homo = same) involving both body and soul: Enrico, the man in the green sweatshirt, is ready to show himself as he is in a city Hannes associated with the light, clarity and sparkling spirit of Mozart's genius. Enrico's risk wins from the dream-ego a decision also to show his body-soul integrity. The dream continues in a rather extraordinary way:

> I am in a huge dimly lit cathedral where Christmas Mass is in progress. The congregation is singing a carol containing reference to the angel of the lord coming down to the shepherds and his glory overwhelming them. As this part is sung, a door opens to the left of the sanctuary and the moon shines in. It is a powerful, awesome experience. The women of the congregation have taken up the singing of the next words. Behind me, an old man, a bit ga-ga, insists on singing along. I look back annoyed as though I want to shut him up with my glance, but he does not see me. Behind this man, in the aisle, stands Enrico. His presence is very reassuring.

The meaning of such a powerful dream is well beyond the scope of this book, but the descent of the angel to earth—to the shepherds!—the resulting glory and the appearance of the moon as the new light of the Mass, all testify to the importance of the union of the yellow with the green man. The green man's reassuring presence seems not only to keep order but also to allow the new Mass related to the matriarchal to unfold.

This change in the green man's appearance—from flower boy to gardener or man-of-the-land—received further comment in a dream Hannes had the following week. Here, the green man was Hannes's friend Willi. In addition to his abilities as an illustrator, Hannes cited Willi's love of home, cooking, and especially gardening, as his first associations. Willi had appeared in several earlier dreams. In one, he conducted Hannes on a tour of his garden where he showed him Easter lilies (renewal) and a delicate white flower on spidery green stems that Hannes found very beautiful. I felt this signified the delicate nature of Hannes's current relationship to the green—something hypersensitive, fledgling. In fact, this dream appeared during a period when Hannes was experiencing a desperate longing for companionship. He felt Willi's flowers and his green thumb gave him hope and reminded him that mere longing does not make a garden grow. The dream about Willi that followed the Enrico images employed the green-yellow vocabulary we had been creating in a direct way:

> I enter Willi's old apartment in B. [hometown], though it doesn't really look that much like it. He greets me very warmly, embracing me and telling me he's so glad I have returned. He wears a greenish-yellow shirt. He conducts me down a long corridor off which several rooms open. They are all

painted in a glowing green, as with Chinese lacquer. The room he has given me to sleep in is also green except for the ceiling which he tells me he has painted yellow just for me.

When he had this dream, Hannes was planning a trip back to B. Willi, as in the previous dream, is the one who shows Hannes what's what. He is a guide, a psychopomp. In reality, Willi has a rather elfin appearance that only reinforces the appropriateness of such a role for him. What he has to show Hannes here is related to an image of home painted in terms of Hannes's still unconscious but rich and glowing greenness. The yellow ceiling reminded us of a very early dream image of a beautiful green ceiling that had "appeal to God." The next part of the dream is even more specific, casting Hannes's search for his own greenness in terms of reunion with his genteel mother's family, with his Catholic and country heritage that father's stern Lutheranism had smothered.

Walking with my mother along a tree-lined street in B., looking for my aunt's house. [The aunt is mother's eldest sister.] I pause before the wrong house. My mother says something like, "No, not that one, the next one." We climb the steps of the porch and knock at the door. The door is green like Willi's apartment and is carved in the middle to resemble a hexagram from the *I Ching*. Aunt Ute answers the door and ushers us into a living room full of light and relatives. It is also the same color as Willi's apartment. I'm a bit uncomfortable with so many relatives and also a bit impatient.

We both felt that such a trip was a necessary excursion to right an imbalance, to effect a reconciliation with an important component of his lost or missing greenness, but that Hannes's impatience signified a recognition that this was not the final stage of his journey or the goal.

In a dream concurrent with the writing of this chapter, Willi is again pointing something out to Hannes, this time from the porch of what looks like a white-washed country cottage in the middle of his former, very urban neighborhood in B. Willi shows him the neighbors also standing on the porch of their country cottage. These neighbors consist of a beautiful dark-haired mother and her three sons aged about fourteen, sixteen and twenty. The boys are carrying a white wicker planter and a picnic supper. They are naked to the waist and the eldest, standing closest to Hannes, has a nicely developed chest. Hannes remarks on his beauty and hopes that the family is going in the same direction as Willi and he. They are not. Hannes is very disappointed. He told me he felt the dream reflected a frequent failing of his not to go where his Eros would lead him. I mention this dream to show again the green man's very practical—but not prosaic—role. His function is, in fact, to awaken, to enlighten the yellow to the possibilities ripe for discovery in the sensual world of nature.

We find the same role accorded green men in the dreams of other yellow men.

Darius, for instance, had the following dream:

A burnt-out Roman site. It's raining. Mist. Several American tourists, young people, poking around. Older men, fathers, too. I introduce these fathers to you [the analyst] as I know you can help them. I begin to walk slowly down a stone ramp with Dieter. He takes me by the hand very tenderly. I feel as if we were very close again. He begins to tell me about his five girlfriends and how important it is to know how to educate them. I feel very warm toward him.

Dieter was an old companion of Darius from his *Gymnasium* days, with whom Darius had had little contact since. Darius remembered him as down-to-earth, very practical, and very tender, too. He also mentioned Dieter's strong peasant-like mother. In the dream, it is Dieter who teaches him about Eros by means of a homoerotic reconnection; this stands in striking opposition to the burnt out and neurotic world of the fathers represented by the remains of the Imperial Roman fortress.

A solid Swiss man with a knowledge of bulldozers, of moving earth and of practical house construction proves the perfect collaborator for Lukas in a dream where he wants to build a house for himself outside the city walls. In another dream, Lukas projected onto me the yellow man and onto a wood-working acquaintance the green:

I go to G.'s new house. He is living on the roof. He is going to rent me a flat. I have brought Martin. I hope G. doesn't mind. G. gives him the flat under the roof and me the one under that. G. is in the process of renovating this flat. Martin pitches in and makes a wooden pedestal for his stereo cabinet. The wood is ash. Martin also tries to repair the ash paneling which has been scarred on one side by a machine plane. G. comes in with his food which he doesn't keep up on the roof because of the sun. I wonder why G. doesn't throw out an old sandy-colored sofa of the 1890s. It has holes in it. But I know he doesn't like to throw anything away.

What is especially interesting about this dream is that the yellow provides the space for the green to flourish and so acts in his visionary capacity—the man on the roof living close to the sun is, of course, the shaman—as a container for the green. This is emphasized by the figure's sensitivity to the food. It is in this space, where the green and yellow collaborate, that Lukas's process can unfold. I felt that the old sofa, to which Lukas associated his Viennese grandparents and the Vienna of the Secession, referred to Freud's beginnings with depth psychology and to the need of continuing with our investigation of the part played by Lukas's past, his infantile wishes, in his present difficulties. Lukas's desire to escape, yellow-man fashion, into a dream world is opposed by a greener Freudian handling.

For Corneliu, the green man is a muscular working-class black man in a sky-blue T-shirt patterned in lines of hammers and sickles. It is not surprising, I think, that such a figure, whose physical force, sensuality and even passion (Corneliu's associations) are covered over with heady (sky-blue) ideology (hammers and sickles), should refuse to cooperate with the dreamer and tell him where his father is: it is the abused green man's passive-aggressive defense.

We have seen that leading the yellow man into life is a specialty of the green man. When the yellow man appears in the dreams of the green, his role is often the same except that the quality of life he reveals is much less physical or sensual. I don't have many examples of green men's dreams—and none of Nino's; perhaps green men do not seek therapy as a resolution to their problems as frequently as do yellow. The flower boy/gardener, Thierry, is an exception. A dream of his offers a most revealing portrait of the yellow man's brand of assistance:

> I am in my apartment with a forty-year-old "marginal" type of man in rumpled clothes. We are in bed together. I get up to make him a coffee and find that he has put up a mobile above my kitchen counter. I like it a lot. I return to bed and think I should thank him by sucking him off, but I don't want to and he doesn't mind. We fall asleep and when I awaken I notice that the curtain at the head of my bed has been repaired so that instead of having to take it down every time I want to look out, it slides along a curtain rod. I am delighted.

To both the mobile and the repaired curtain arrangement Thierry associated "light." Over the months we returned to this dream often, both of us recognizing the transference issues it raised.

In Willi's dreams, light is also frequently associated with the yellow man.

> In the late afternoon, I stand admiring the Seine and the city of Paris from the Pont des Arts. Hannes comes along and we enthuse on the subject of the beauty of Paris in the fall. We then wander through the winding streets near the university, grocery shopping in wonderful little French shops.

When I asked Willi for his association to Paris, he immediately exclaimed, "Light!" Just as Willi was for Hannes an appropriate figure to introduce him to the meaning of greenness, so Hannes and his yellow capacity for articulating and making connections, is a perfect companion for Willi through the *Ville Lumière*. He helps Willi to see the relationship between art as a spiritual phenomenon and artisanship (Willi's illustrations, his garden, his meals). If we listen to another dream of Paris from Willi, following the first by ten days, we get a further sense of the meaning of light in the green man's tasks:

> I and a group of people have taken over an old house in Paris. The interior walls are white old-fashioned slat walls. A white outdoors fence runs along the inside walls of the place and the floors are edged with grass: a two-foot border with a hardwood centre. The wooden part of the floor looks like a rug with its grassy, floor edge. We seem to be clearing and exploring the house.

There is no furniture as yet. A gate on the fence is removed and laid horizontally on boards to make a bench.

While for Hannes, losing himself in the sensuality of lush gardens—with or without beautiful men—seems to be desirable, with Willi it is rather a question of pushing those gardens to the walls, claiming human ground from nature, creating a man-made standpoint—using nature to make that ground, but in such a way that Willi has a conscious say. The *Ville Lumière* is after all a moving testimony to such efforts.

One other major feature of Hannes's unconscious world we cannot overlook was the frequent presence of his sister Sylvie. She appeared more often than any other person except Nino. Her earthiness, sensuality, practicality, and even her adolescent amorality, offer some explanation. These are qualities she shares with Nino. On more than one occasion, she and Nino even swapped identities in Hannes's dreams, with one turning easily into the other. Symbolically, the chief difference between Sylvie and Nino, as in the Melanesian brother and sister pair, lies in Sylvie's indivisibility from her brother; she is his "natural fertility,"[329] while Nino represents the desirable fertility of the Other.

I have already mentioned the important symbolic role the sister of the yellow man (and of the green man, too, though less frequently) plays in such myths as that of Orestes and Pylades or in fiction like Forster's *Maurice*. She is one expression of the affectional bond between yellow and green and/or she is an anima-Muse inspiring resolution of the green-yellow dialogue. The sister of golden-boy Darius could be said to take the former role, at least in life. In dreams, she often serves as a female counterpart to Darius's Apollonian blondness. Blonde women resembling the sister also appear frequently in erotic entanglements with him, and, on occasion, he shares the blonde sister-woman with a dark-haired, sexually potent man, whom I would call Dionysian.

Sister-like women, if not sister herself, heavily populated the dreams of the painter Corneliu as well. Here their role was more guide and Muse than bonding agent. The first dream Corneliu brought to analysis was, in fact, of an older sister (unknown) in a white dress spotted with red and blue flowers. She was standing in a green field proudly displaying her swollen belly. Corneliu thought she might be eight months' pregnant. This image of the feminine struck me as just right for a creative yellow man. The child she gave birth to carried traits of Corneliu's need to commit himself to his painting as well as of his need to honor his sexuality without apology.

Hannes's dream of his pregnant sister seemed also to be pointing to his creative fullness, at a time when the question of not only bearing but also caring

---

[329] Herdt, *Ritualized Homosexuality,* p. 354.

for his greenness was ripe. However, here the child is paralleled with the gift of the green man himself:

> After what seems like a difficult childbirth, my sister is delivered of a little baby that in spite of its size weighs in at eight pounds. I am the father and absolutely delighted with the child. I put it up to its mother's breast to suckle. My sister wears a silver cross around her bare throat. A male friend gives me a gift of an emerald in a round silver setting. Once my sister is on her feet again, she declares that she's not really cut out to be a mother, so I have complete charge of the child.

The green stone in its feminine silver setting is a clear expression, I feel, of a greater collective issue involving the masculine's acceptance of its own feminine duties. That acceptance is one of the gifts the green man brings to the yellow. The emerald stone, like the Grail a symbol of wholeness or Self, is every bit the equivalent, indeed the companion, of the child.

Halfway through the analysis Hannes made contact with Nino. Both were embarrassed, Nino by the brutality with which he had broken with Hannes, Hannes by the ugly recriminations he had hurled at Nino's head during and after the break-up. Embarrassment eventually gave way to a desire for friendship. Distance has allowed the new friendship a chance to develop slowly. Hannes finds himself thinking for the first time in years of the possibility of a relationship with someone else. His erotic life has been limited until now as much by his depression over the loss of Nino as by the AIDS scare (a factor that a person as morbidly sensitive to his health and body as Hannes could never view without mild panic).

Not long after Hannes's reunion with Nino, Willi decided to return to B. and Hannes began to think of doing the same—he would transfer his studies to the university there. We discussed his plans at length. He was nervous about returning, even anxious. He would be uprooted again, he said, and he was afraid that his new awareness might cut him off from his old contacts, from his roots. Then he had the following dream which seemed to say that going home was of a piece with the rest of his search for the green:

> I arrive at Nino's with suitcases. It doesn't really look like Nino's. No one is at home except the neighbor downstairs who lets me in and shows me the secret door on the landing that leads up to the bedroom. I go through this door and ascend the stairs to bed. I sleep. After a while Nino appears at the window on a ladder, sunbrowned and dressed for hiking in the country. He is smiling as he climbs through the window into the room. Sobbing, I waken and greet him. . . . Then I wander out of a cluster of dark buildings into open space in company with a dark-haired young man. It is bright and sunny though winter. In front of us to the left is a Neo-Gothic building like a church or the college I attended. My companion and I each have half a fish on a leash. We put the fish back together and continue the path to our right.

As the image of the fish as psychopomp seems to suggest, returning home brings Hannes to both a secular and sacred knowledge of Self, and beyond knowledge to a deep erotic bond with the Other. (It may also bring him companionship, if we interpret the dark-haired young man concretely.)

Several times in the course of the analysis, Hannes's dreams had pointed out a spiritual or numinous meaning in the green. The green ceiling I have already mentioned; but there was also Christ as a rose-gardener, God Himself as green, not to mention a myriad of priests mediating between nature and heaven, bringing them together in a true Johannine fashion. But, in the end, the green ceiling so appealing to God becomes green walls, while the yellow is pushed ceiling-ward again. Even though a late dream showed Hannes opening his mouth to confess his love for a long-admired man and frogs came popping out, he did not become a green man. He strives to make conscious the green power within him seeking expression, but his approach to it must always be that of the yellow man; it is his fate, both blessing and curse. We once had this described for us in a dream as an Anubis-headed symbolist painter from Java prowling a moonlit French garden framed by gravel walks. To go as far as Hannes went in integrating the green, taking it to heart, was, as his very last dream indicated, a torture:

I am strapped to a table against one wall of a basement workroom. The table is attached to some kind of machine that sends vibrations through the table. The warden is a young man with shoulder-length brown hair. One day, while he is wrapping a parcel, the machine goes off. He does not come to turn it back on as I would expect, but finishes the packing and then leaves the room to post the package. I know that I am at last free to get up. Suddenly, Paolo [a dancer in Zürich Hannes knew and liked] comes into the room and leads me out through another door along white corridors. Finally we go up a flight of stairs past a garden courtyard like that at the art gallery into an airport lounge. Paolo tells me he has arranged my homeward flight. I see a plane with a red tail. I ask him if he is coming with me. He says, "No, I can't." But he puts his arms around my neck and his legs around my waist and abruptly changes into a silver medallion in, not on, my chest. The medallion shows an eighteenth-century shepherd, some trees and a sheep.

Hannes said little about this dream except to confirm the struggle it had been to own even a piece of green for himself and to admit he saw no other way of reaching his ground, his home. The green man had to be owned.

Observations

Hannes of course represents an extreme case of the yellow man and his relationship to Nino an extreme example of the creative—and destructive—interplay of green and yellow in a homoerotic setting. Of the other cases cited, only Darius and Willi—golden boy and gardener, respectively—manifest similar extremes. The others are mixes. Thierry, for instance, longing for his home in the country where he could divide his time between translating and editorial work on the one side and looking after plants and animals on the other, is clearly a mix of green and red, with red, I would say, predominating. (I am linking red with translation and editorial work, which serves the creative artist but is not fundamentally creative or artistic.)

However, to reiterate what I said earlier, it is only when men engage one another along the green-yellow axis that something truly creative takes place between them. Yellow and green not only fit together as contained to container, but also infiltrate each other's domains; they ignite to flame up and deepen, spiraling to the heavens and plunging into the bowels of the earth—the movements are paradoxically simultaneous. With artists, this green-yellow dialogue is a kind of mother tongue.

In the creative homoerotic exchange, one or, more often, both partners are required at different times to play the green role and so the masculine is always brought to an acknowledgment of its own greenness or links to green. Even in our so-called advanced culture, the green quality remains largely repressed, exploited and despised, mainly because of its ties to the Great Mother.

The mad embracing of a Dionysian/Priapic green which defined the homosexual scene in Western cities during the 1970s is not, of course, what I am talking about here. That movement, understandable enough in light of decades of puritanical repression, was as abusive and exploitative of the green power as what preceded it, only in a different way. Dionysian erotic madness was after all a sacred affair; glinting behind the orgies of the bathhouses and back-room bars was only the gold-toothed leer of that old god, Capital—soul was sold for instant gratification.

Clearly absent from this collective drive into a split-off, undersold green was the yellow man's illuminating abilities. These were not allowed to shine in places priding themselves on their obscurity. In perfect keeping with the old puritanical position, yellow was reserved for "better," nobler things than the body and its embarrassing demands.

Only when green and yellow are encouraged to come together as they are meant to—to inspire and challenge each other—will that liberation take place that the Uranians spoke of a century ago (and which every champion of male-male Eros ever since has echoed). Such a liberation will doubtless reverberate throughout the whole culture, for the green-yellow split has haunted all of us since the arrival of the first sun god on the verdant horizon of the matriarchal world.

Bibliography

Aeschylus. *The Oresteia.* London: Penguin Books, 1981.

Alain-Fournier, Henri. *Le grand Meaulnes.* Lausanne: J. Marquerat, 1953.

Alexander, Marc. *British Folklore.* New York: Crescent Books, 1982.

Andersen, Hans Christian. *Ardizzone's Hans Andersen: Fourteen Classic Tales.* London: André Deutsch, 1978.

Austen, Jane. *Pride and Prejudice.* London: Penguin Books, 1985.

Balint, Michael. *The Basic Fault: Therapeutic Aspects of Regression.* New York: Brunner/Mazel, Inc., 1979.

Beebe, John. "Toward an Image of Male Partnership." *Psychological Perspectives,* vol. 23 (Fall 1990).

Beltz, Walter. *God and the Gods: Myths of the Bible.* Harmondsworth: Penguin Books, 1983.

Boswell, John. *Christianity, Social Tolerance and Homosexuality.* Chicago: University of Chicago Press, 1980.

Byron, Lord. *The Poetical Works of Lord Byron.* London: Oxford University Press, 1966.

Call, F.O. *In a Belgian Garden and Other Poems.* London: E. MacDonald, 1917.

Campbell, Michael. *Lord Dismiss Us.* Chicago: U. of Chicago Press, 1984.

Carpenter, Edward. *Selected Writings,* v. 1. London: GMP, 1984.

_____, ed. *Ioläus: An Anthology of Friendship.* London: Allen & Unwin, 1929.

Cecil, David. *A Portrait of Jane Austen.* Harmondsworth: Penguin Books, 1980.

Chevalier, Jean and Gheerbrandt, Alain. *Dictionnaire des Symboles.* Paris: Editions Robert Laffont, 1982.

Cocea, N.D. *Le vin de longue vie.* Aix-en-Provence: Alinea, 1989.

Cooper, Emmanuel. *The Life and Work of Henry Scott Tuke, 1858-1929.* London: GMP, 1987.

D'Arch Smith, Timothy. *Love in Earnest.* London: Routledge & Kegan Paul, 1970.

Davidson, Gustav. *A Dictionary of Angels: Including the Fallen Angels.* New York: Free Press, 1967.

Dixon, H.P. "In Memoriam," on *Songs by Finzi and His Friends.* Hyperion Records, 1981.

Dorment, Richard, et al. *Alfred Gilbert: Sculptor and Goldsmith.* London: Royal Academy of Arts, 1986.

Dover, K.J. *Greek Homosexuality.* New York: Vintage Books, 1980.

Euripides. *Orestes and Other Plays.* London: Penguin Books, 1972.

_____. *Three Plays: Alcestis, Hippolytus, Iphigenia in Tauris.* London: Penguin Books, 1974.

Fernandez, Dominique. *Le rapt de Ganymède.* Paris: Bernard Grasset, 1989.

Figes, Eva. *Light.* New York: Ballantine Books, 1984.

Findley, Timothy. *The Wars.* Markham, Ont.: Penguin Books, 1978.

Firbank, Ronald. *Valmouth.* London: Duckworth, 1977.

Fitzgerald, Edward, trans. *The Rubáiyát of Omar Khayyam.* London: Collins, n.d.

Forster, E.M. *The Life to Come and Other Stories.* Harmondsworth: Penguin Books, 1975.

Forster, E.M. *Maurice.* London: Penguin Books, 1987.

Frazer, Sir James. *The Golden Bough.* New York: Macmillan, 1963.

Furbank, P.N. *E.M. Forster: A Life.* Oxford: Oxford University Press, 1977.

Fussell, Paul. *The Great War and Modern Memory.* New York: Oxford University Press, 1977.

Gardner, Brian. *The Terrible Rain: The War Poets, 1939-1945.* London: Methuen, 1983.

Gathorne-Hardy, Jonathan. *The Old School Tie: The Phenomenon of the English Public School.* New York: The Viking Press, 1978.

Genet, Jean. *Haute surveillance.* Paris: Gallimard, 1988.

Gide, André. *The Immoralist.* Trans. Richard Howard. New York: Alfred A. Knopf, 1970.

_____. *Saül.* Paris: Gallimard, 1942.

Giono, Jean. *The Man Who Planted Trees.* London: Peter Owen, 1989.

Goethe, J.W. *Theory of Colours.* London: John Murray, 1840.

Graves, Robert. *Greek Myths.* London: Penguin Books, 1984.

Green, Julien. *Sud.* Paris: Le Livre de Poche, 1968.

Green, Richard. *The "Sissy Boy" Syndrome and the Development of Homosexuality.* New Haven: Yale University Press, 1987.

The Complete Grimm's Fairy Tales. New York: Pantheon Books, 1944.

Hamilton, Edith. *Mythology.* New York: New American Library, 1969.

Handl, Irene. *The Gold Tip Pfitzer.* London: Fontana Paperbacks, 1987.

Hannah, Barbara. *Striving Towards Wholeness.* New York: G.P. Putnam's Sons, 1971.

Harding, M. Esther. *Woman's Mysteries: Ancient and Modern.* New York: Harper & Row, 1971.

Harrison, G.B., comp. *A Book of British Poetry: Chaucer to Rossetti.* London: Penguin Books, 1953.

Herdt, Gilbert, et al. *Ritualized Homosexuality in Melanesia.* Berkeley: University of California Press, 1984.

_____. *Rituals of Manhood: Male Initiation in Papua New Guinea.* Berkeley: University of California Press, 1982.

Hetrick, Emery S. and Stein, Terry S. *Innovations in Psychotherapy with Homosexuals.* Washington D.C.: American Psychiatric Press Inc., 1984.

Hildegard von Bingen. *Illuminations of Hildegard of Bingen.* Santa Fe: Bear & Co., Inc., 1985.

Hill, Susan. *The Bird of Night.* London: Penguin Books, 1976.

_____. *Strange Meeting.* Harmondsworth: Penguin Books, 1974.

Hillman, James, et al. *Puer Papers.* Dallas: Spring Publications, 1979.

The Holy Bible. Revised Standard Version, Catholic Edition. London: Catholic Truth Society, 1966.

Homer. *The Illiad.* New York: Airmont Publishing Company Inc., 1966.

Hopcke, Robert. *Jung, Jungians and Homosexuality.* Boston: Shambhala Publications, 1988.

Horner, Tom. *Jonathan Loved David: Homosexuality in Biblical Times.* Philadelphia: The Westminster Press, 1978.

Housman, A.E. *A Shropshire Lad.* London: Harrap, 1984.

Hunt, Chris. *Street Lavendar.* London: GMP, 1986.

Ihara, Saikaku. *Comrade Loves of the Samurai.* Tokyo: Chas. E. Tuttle Co., 1972.

Istrati, Panait. *Kyra Kyralina.* Freeport, N.Y.: Books for Libraries Press, 1971.

Jackson, Holbrook. *The Eighteen Nineties.* London: The Cresset Library, 1988.

Johnston, Jennifer. *The Captains and the Kings.* London: Fontana, 1985.

——. *How Many Miles to Babylon?* Glasgow: Fontana Paperbacks, 1981.

Jullian, Philippe. *Dreamers of Decadence: Symbolist Painters of the 1890's.* New York: Praeger Publishers, 1971.

Jung, C.G. *The Collected Works of C.G. Jung* (Bollingen Series XX). 20 vols. Trans. R.F.C. Hull. Ed. H. Read, M. Fordham, G. Adler, Wm. McGuire. Princeton: Princeton University Press, 1953-1979.

——. *The Freud/Jung Letters* (Bollingen Series XCIV). Trans. Ralph Manheim, R.F.C. Hull. Ed. Wm. McGuire. Princeton: Princeton University Press, 1974.

Kendall, Elizabeth. *Where She Danced.* New York: Alfred A. Knopf, 1979.

Kureishi, Hanif. *My Beautiful Laundrette* and *The Rainbow Sign.* London: Faber & Faber, 1986.

Lang, A., ed. *The Crimson Fairy Book.* New York: Dover Publications Inc., 1969.

——. *The Violet Fairy Book.* New York: Dover Publications Inc., 1966.

Lopez-Pedraza, Rafael. *Hermes and His Children.* Zurich: Spring Publications, 1977.

Mackintosh, Alastair. *Symbolism and Art Nouveau.* London: Thames & Hudson, 1975.

Mann, Thomas. *Death in Venice and Seven Other Stories.* New York: Vintage Books, 1936.

Mason, Herbert. *Gilgamesh: A Verse Narrative.* New York: NAL, 1972.

Mayne, Xavier. *Imre: A Memorandum.* New York: Arno Press, 1975.

Meeker, Richard. *Better Angel.* Boston: Alyson Publications Inc., 1989.

Melville, Herman. *Redburn.* Harmondsworth: Penguin Books, 1977.

Michell, John. *The Earth Spirit: Its Ways, Shrines and Mysteries.* London: Thames & Hudson, 1975.

Mindell, Arnold. *Dream Body: The Body's Role in Revealing the Self.* London: Routledge & Kegan Paul, 1984.

Mishima, Yukio. *Confessions of a Mask.* New York: New Directions, 1958.

Monick, Eugene. *Phallos: Sacred Image of the Masculine.* Toronto: Inner City Books, 1987.

Montherlant, Henri de. *La ville dont le prince est un enfant.* Paris: Gallimard, 1967.

Mulock, Dinah Maria. *John Halifax, Gentleman.* London: Dent, 1906.

Navarre, Yves. *Le petit galopin de nos corps.* Paris: Robert Laffont, 1977.

Neumann, Erich. *The Child.* London: Hodder & Stoughton, 1973.

_____. *The Origins and History of Consciousness* (Bollingen Series XLII). Princeton: Princeton University Press, 1970.

Ovid. *Metamorphoses.* Oxford: Oxford University Press, 1986.

Owen, Wilfred. *The Poems of Wilfred Owen.* London: The Hogarth Press, 1985.

Parsons, I.M., ed. *Men Who March Away: Poems of the First World War.* Toronto: Clarke, Irwin & Company Ltd., 1966.

Pater, Walter. *The Renaissance.* Oxford: Oxford University Press, 1986.

Penna, Sandro. *Tutte le poesie.* Milano: Garzanti Editore, 1977.

Plato. *Phædrus and the Seventh and Eighth Letters.* Harmondsworth: Penguin Books, 1973.

_____. *The Symposium.* London: Penguin Books, 1952.

Read, Benedict. *Victorian Sculpture.* London: Yale University Press, 1982.

Rees, David. *In the Tent.* Boston: Alyson Publications Inc., 1985.

Reid, Forrest. *The Garden God: A Tale of Two Boys.* London: David Nutt, 1906.

_____. *Uncle Stephen.* London: GMP, 1988.

_____. *Young Tom.* London: GMP, 1987.

Renault, Mary. *The Charioteer.* London: Sceptre Books, 1986.

Reynolds, Simon. *The Vision of Simeon Solomon.* Stroud, Gloc.: Catalpa Press Ltd., 1984.

Rosenfels, Paul. *Homosexuality: The Psychology of the Creative Process.* New York: Ninth St. Center, Inc., 1986.

Saba, Umberto. *Ernesto.* Manchester: Carcanet, 1987.

Sadi of Shiraz, Sheikh Muslihuh-din. *The Rose Garden.* London: Octagon , 1979.

Salomon, Jacques. *Auprès de Vuillard.* Paris: La Palme, 1953.

Samuels, Andrew, et al. *A Critical Dictionary of Jungian Analysis.* London: Routledge & Kegan Paul, 1986.

Samuelson, Peter. *Post-War Friends: Paintings & Drawings.* London: GMP, 1987.

Schellenbaum, Peter. *How to Say No to the One You Love: The Role of Boundaries in Relationships.* Wilmette, Ill.: Chiron Publications, 1987.

Scott, Ian A. *The Lüscher Color Test.* New York: Washington Square Press, 1971.

Sergent, Bernard. *L'homosexualité initiatique dans l'Europe ancienne.* Paris: Payot, 1986.

_____. *Homosexuality in Greek Myth.* Boston: Beacon Press, 1986.

Service, Alastair. *Edwardian Architecture: A Handbook to Building Design in Britain 1890-1914.* London: Thames & Hudson, 1978.

Shakespeare, William. *Henry V.* London: Penguin Books, 1968.

_____. *The Sonnets.* London: Dent, 1976.

Sheen, Fulton J. *The Seven Last Words.* New York: Alba House, 1982.

Sherriff, R.C. *Journey's End.* London: Penguin Books, 1983.

Stallings, Laurence, ed. *The First World War: A Photographic History.* London: Daily Express, 1933.

Stevens, Anthony. *Archetype: A Natural History of the Self.* London: Routledge & Kegan Paul, 1982.

Sutherland, Alistair and Anderson, Patrick. *Eros: An Anthology of Male Friendship.* New York: The Citadel Press, 1968.

Taylor, Martin. *Lads: Love Poetry of the Trenches.* London: Constable, 1989.

Tennyson, Alfred. *In Memoriam, Maud and Other Poems.* London: Dent, 1974.

Thompson, Mark. *Gay Spirit: Myth and Meaning.* New York: St. Martin's, 1987.

Traherne, Thomas. *Selected Writings.* Manchester: Carcanet, 1988.

Tripp, C.A. *The Homosexual Matrix.* New York: McGraw-Hill, 1975.

Tuchmann, Barbara W. *The Proud Tower: A Portrait of the World before the War, 1890-1914.* Toronto: Bantam, 1967.

Ungaretti, Giuseppe. *Selected Poems.* Trans. Patrick Creagh. Harmondsworth: Penguin Books, 1971.

Vannier, Dr. Léon. *La typologie et ses applications thérapeutiques.* Paris: Doin Editeurs, 1976.

Verlaine, Paul. *La bonne chanson, Romance sans paroles, Sagesse.* Paris: Le livre de poche, 1963.

Virgil. *The Eclogues.* London: Penguin Books, 1987.

Vries, Ad de. *Dictionary of Symbols and Imagery.* Amsterdam: North-Holland Publishing Co., 1976.

Warner, Marina. *The Crack in the Teacup: Britain in the 20th Century.* London: André Deutsch, 1979.

Whitman, Walt. *The Complete Poems.* London: Penguin Books, 1986.

Wiener, Martin. *English Culture and the Decline of the Industrial Spirit. 1850-1980.* Harmondsworth: Penguin Books, 1985.

Wilde, Oscar. *Complete Shorter Fiction.* Oxford: Oxford University Press, 1980.

_____. *Complete Works of Oscar Wilde.* London: Collins, 1966.

Williams, Tennessee. *In the Winter of Cities.* New York: New Directions, 1956.

Williams, Walter L. *The Spirit and the Flesh: Sexual Diversity in American Indian Culture.* Boston: Beacon Press, 1986.

Wilson, Annie and Bek, Lilla. *What Colour are You?* Northhamptonshire: The Aquarian Press, 1981.

Winnicott, D.W. *Playing and Reality.* Harmondsworth: Penguin Books, 1985.

Wyly, James. *The Phallic Quest: Priapus and Masculine Inflation.* Toronto: Inner City Books, 1989.

Yourcenar, Marguerite. *Coup de Grâce.* London: Black Swan Books, 1984.

_____. *Fires.* London: Black Swan Books, 1985.

Zilinsky, Ursula. *The Long Afternoon.* London: W.H. Allen, 1984.

_____. *Middle Ground.* London: GMP, 1987.

Index

154

Studies in Jungian Psychology
by Jungian Analysts

Sewn Paperbacks